How to Break 90– Consistently!

How to Break 90– Consistently!

by FRANK CHINNOCK
Illustrated by ED VEBELL

J. B. LIPPINCOTT COMPANY
Philadelphia & New York

U.S. Library of Congress Cataloging in Publication Data

Chinnock, Frank W   birth date
How to break 90—consistently!

1. Golf. I. Title.
GV965.C476   796.352′3   76–22655
ISBN–0–397–01118–0

Contents

Introduction

In *How to Break 90—Consistently*, I have tried to write a book for those golfers who need it the most: the millions of dedicated yet frustrated hackers who every Saturday or Sunday brave rain, crowds, cold winds, and man-made hazards to try to play the maddening game called golf.

Most golf books have been written by (or ghostwritten for) top touring professionals and are designed to increase your drives from 230 to 260 yards, or to make your swing "a thing of beauty to behold." Yet over the years, I have found that the vast majority of golfers want just two things on the golf course: *not* to make damn fools of themselves in front of others, and to have a little—just a little—fun and relaxation.

To help them achieve these modest, yet somehow unobtainable goals, I have gone not to a "name" pro, but to the country-club professionals in my own area. For those are the men who, day after day, have to deal with the problems and complaints of the weekend golfer who is inevitably a high-handicap player. Over many years of teaching, these club pros have perfected certain techniques and methods of in-

7

struction to help their members lower their scores. In this book, they pass along their proven stroke-saving tips to you. So, when I refer to a "pro" in the book, I'm talking about one of these men.

The purpose of these tips is to help you break 90, and it is no accident or whim that the figure of 90 was chosen. For, of the estimated 12 million golfers in the United States who play at least three rounds of golf a year, reliable figures reveal that only *4 percent* can break 90 consistently. That means that one hell of a lot of divots are flying through the air every weekend.

Women golfers can use these tips just as easily as men— and they already start off with one big advantage. All of my country-club professionals agreed that slowing down your swing was essential to improving your game. And almost without exception women instinctively swing more slowly than men. Maybe it's because they are in no hurry to get back to their housework.

As for left-handed golfers, all they have to do is reverse the instructions. But they've undoubtedly heard that so often that they're probably reading this sentence from right to left.

Forget about trying to match Jack Nicklaus's drive or Gene Littler's irons. Set your goals realistically. Remember, the aim is to break 90—and get yourself in that exclusive 4 percent bracket. So, if you are one of those 11,520,000 up-tight golfers for whom the magic figure of 89 is your personal Mt. Everest, this book is meant for you.

fwc

1

Enter Harvey, Swinging

Golf: "*A game which consists in striking a small, resilient ball with clubs having heads into a series of holes situated at varying distances on a course with natural or artificial hazards irregularly interposed.*"—*Webster's Dictionary.*

Idiot: "*Anyone who plays golf.*"—*Wife of almost any golfer.*

I first met Harvey Hacker about six months ago. "Hacker" is not his real name, but after our initial round of golf together, I couldn't think of him any other way. Harvey was pushing fifty, a bit overweight, overpaunched, overstrained, and over the hill when it came to physical fitness. He was about 5 feet 10, balding, with an ever-present cigar clamped viselike in his jaws. He also had quite a temper, but all I saw in the beginning was his jovial grin.

We met on the first tee of a Westchester County public golf course on a Monday morning in April. It was one of the first warm days of the young year, and I had taken off and headed for the links. That's one of the advantages of being a writer. If you're at all conscientious (which means if you've developed the habit of eating three times a day), and you're a golf nut at the same time, you get into the habit of putting in your hours at the typewriter on a Saturday or Sunday. Then you can play golf on Monday when it doesn't take you seven or eight hours to get around the course.

Harvey was swinging a driver, not easy, relaxed, warm-up swings, but as though he were trying to kill a bee—vicious, angry swipes at some imaginary object. He looked up as I approached.

"Hi there. Playing alone?"

"Yes."

"Good. Wanna join up?"

"Fine."

"Name's Harvey." He stuck out a big hand, and when I shook it, I knew that this was a strong man. Not that he tried to weld my fingers together, but I could feel the latent power there.

"I'm Frank."

He took a couple of more swings, then asked, ever so casually, "What do you shoot?"

I shrugged. "It depends. I don't play often enough to have a reliable handicap. But I'll probably be somewhere in the eighties."

He sighed. "I thought we might have a little wager, but I'm not in that category. I'll be lucky if I break a hundred," he added grimly.

"Let's just play a friendly round. Why don't you show me the way?"

He teed up and addressed the ball. I couldn't help noticing how far away from it he stood, his arms straining forward, bent way over at the waist, his weight on his toes. His backswing was so fast it was a blur, but the smack of the ball was no illusion. It started out high over the left rough, sliced back across the fairway, and ended up about 220 yards in the right rough. With that slice, I was amazed he got so much distance. He had to be very strong indeed.

"That'll play," I said and teed up my own ball. I took a few practice swings to get a little looser, determined not to try to kill the ball. I did swing easily and made sweet-part-of-the-club contact. The ball went out straight, almost lazily, and rolled to a stop in the middle of the fairway about 20 yards short of Harvey's ball.

"Nice and straight," he said, obviously not very impressed with my length off the tee.

The first hole was relatively easy, not too narrow and only 355 yards long. The green was well trapped, both in front and on the sides.

I was away and when I reached my ball, I studied the shot I had left. Ordinarily, and with no wind, I would hit a 6-iron from that spot. But I was still not fully warmed up and there was trouble in front of the green, not behind it. There was a slight left-to-right crosswind, so I hit a 5-iron toward the left-hand side of the green. The wind pushed the ball a bit, and it landed and held on the fat part of the green.

"Nice shot," said Harvey. "You sure do swing easy." The way he said it, it didn't sound like a compliment.

When we reached Harvey's ball, he immediatcly selected what appeared to be a 9-iron. From where he was, in the rough and from that distance, there was no way I could have reached the green with a 9-iron. Still, as I had noted, he was very strong.

Again, there was that fast backswing, and he hit the ground about 4 inches behind the ball. A plate of grass sailed some 10 yards. The ball had not moved.

Harvey's jaws tightened on the cigar and he swung again. This time he hit the ball on the toe of the club, and it skittered at right angles into the underbrush. Harvey man-

11

aged to get out in two, but caught the trap in front of the green. He wasted two more in there, got on the green, and three-putted. Meanwhile, I had lagged to about 2 feet and made the short putt for my four.

"What shall I put you down for?" I asked Harvey.

"Gimme a ten," he growled. I didn't say anything.

The second hole was a par-five. The fairway went out about 180 yards, then doglegged sharply to the left. From that point on there were about 340 yards to the green.

It was my honor, so I pulled out a 3-iron, hit it cleanly down the middle, and ended up in perfect position for my second shot.

I was sure Harvey would hit an iron, too. The structure of the hole almost demanded it. But out came the driver once more.

Harvey saw me eyeing it and said, "I'm gonna take the short way. If I really catch one, I can clear those trees, cut the dogleg, and save a hundred yards. Might even get home in two."

Again, I didn't say anything. But I was thinking of the thousands of disastrous shots that must have been preceded by the words, "If I really catch one," or something similar.

Harvey took a tremendous swing, but he hit only the top half of the ball. It never rose above 10 feet, and it was still at that height when it disappeared into the woods. We couldn't see the ball anymore, but we could certainly hear it —tick, tock, tick, tock—as it bounced off trees. Harvey took an 11 on that hole. I mishit my second shot but still got my bogey six.

The third hole had a parallel hazard, a stream running alongside the right rough. I played my tee shot well to the left. Harvey took another mighty swing at the ball—and missed it completely. He stood glaring down at the innocent white instrument of his torment. Then he stepped a little closer to the ball, swung, and hit it flush. The ball screamed out about 190 yards. Then it seemed to meet a traffic cop, arms upraised, for the ball turned very sharply to the right, sailed over the rough, and into the stream. When Harvey flung his driver, it went only 40 yards. But it was in the middle of the fairway.

On the next hole, par-four, 410 yards, Harvey and I were both in the right rough on our drives. We were still 200 yards away from the green, both with a bad lie. I pulled out my 5-iron, made sure to hit the ball first, not the ground, and it stopped about 50 yards away from the green.

Harvey, looking scornfully at me, yanked out his 3-wood. He topped it about 15 yards, stalked to where it lay, still in the rough, and swung his wood again. Another top. Now he was about 160 yards away, but he had reached the fairway. He hit a 5-iron and pulled it into the left-hand trap. Three to get out of the trap and two putts for a nine.

In the meantime, I had hit a nice easy half-9-iron and had been lucky enough to sink my 15-foot putt for a four.

As we walked away from the green, Harvey asked, "You had a par there, didn't you?" His expression was puzzled.

"Yes. I was playing for my bogey, but the putt dropped."

"Playing for your bogey?" He was still puzzled.

I tried to explain. "Look, Harvey, I was lying in the rough in a bad lie two hundred yards away, same as you. My chances of hitting a perfect three-wood from that spot were maybe one in ten. On the other hand, my chances of hitting an easy five-iron cleanly were at least five out of ten. You play poker, don't you?" When he nodded, I went on. "Well, if your chances of filling a straight were one out of ten, and your chances of getting a pair were fifty-fifty, what would you go for?"

13

"The pair," he said at once.

"Then why did you defy the odds on the golf course? Why did you hit the low percentage shot back there?"

"That's different. I thought I could make the green."

"You *wished* you could make the green," I corrected. "If you'd really *thought*, you would have known that your chances of actually doing it were very slim. Why didn't you just lay up close and pitch on? Even if you two-putted, you would have made your bogey."

"But that's no fun," he protested.

"Harvey, I had a four," I said softly. "Do you really think that getting a nine on that hole is *fun?*"

He looked thoughtful, but I didn't think I had convinced him.

I was right. The next few holes were more of the same. Harvey played a couple of them well, but the overall result was discouraging: four, eight, seven, five, nine. The madder Harvey got, the more viciously he swung and the worse the results. I kept my mouth shut, not wanting a driver wrapped around my head.

The volcano finally erupted on the tenth hole, a 205-yard par three, with water in front of the green. I hit a good 4-wood and ended up 40 feet from the pin.

"What did you hit?" he asked.

"A four-wood, and I hit it real good."

He shook his head. "I don't need that much club. I can make it with a four-iron."

He hit the iron fairly well, but it was slicing and that cut down the distance. Into the water. He hit another one with the same club. Into the water. Another one. This time it was a shank. And the volcano blew. First, the language, then the clubs, one by one.

When it was over, he turned to me, his face red and

furious. "I've had this Goddamn game. That's the last time. I quit."

"Oh, it's not that bad, Harvey. You'll get over it."

"It *is* that bad, and I *won't* get over it. That's the last round of golf I play. What's the use of torturing myself?"

"Well, if it's really torture . . ."

"Look, for years I worked my ass off, week after week. I'd play golf on Saturday or Sunday for fun. For *fun*, for Christ's sake! But by the fourth or fifth hole, after a bunch of nines, tens, and elevens, my whole day was ruined. All I wanted to do was play passable golf like other people do. And all I did was make a fool of myself."

"You're not alone, Harvey. Do you know that of the twelve million people who play golf, only forty percent of them have ever broken a hundred? That means there are some seven million golfers who are in your boat."

"Somehow that just doesn't make me feel any better. You know I'm a pretty good bowler and a good swimmer. I'm good at my job and I'm no dummy. But I'm so damn stupid at this game. It's not worth it. I used to play with some guys on weekends, but I got so bad I had to beg off. The way I was playing was embarrassing. It was humiliating. I was ashamed even to be on the course with those guys."

"You ever think about taking some lessons?"

"Lessons?" He sounded surprised at the very idea.

"Yes, lessons. People take lessons to ski, to swim, to play tennis, in fact, for almost everything except golf. They seem to think that it doesn't matter how you hit the ball as long as you hit it. What they soon find out—what you have found out—is that they're always hitting more bad shots than good ones. Lessons can turn that around—lessons and practice."

"Well, I did think of taking a few lessons, but . . ." He

15

paused and sighed deeply. "I'll tell you the way it is, Frank. I just acquired a partner in my business, which means that I can now relax a little, take some time off. I considered taking some lessons. But let's face it. You can't teach an old dog new tricks. I'm fifty years old and I've been hacking around for over twenty years. At this late stage, no one's going to start from scratch and give me a beautiful new swing. And I don't expect it. All I really want is some basic tips, some advice on how I can play this game without making a complete ass of myself."

"You mean you want to be able to hit the ball solid enough to get a little 'feel'?"

"That's it exactly." He nodded vigorously.

I thought for a moment. Why not? The idea was certainly worth proposing to him.

"Harvey, how would you like to be able to break ninety?"

"Ninety?" He looked at me incredulously. "You've seen me play. As far as I'm concerned, breaking ninety is like reaching the moon in a golf cart. I'd be delirious if I could even break a hundred every now and then."

"I said ninety. And I don't mean every now and then. I mean regularly."

"I'd do anything," he said fervently. "Anything. Ninety! Jesus!"

"Then I think I can help you."

"You? How?"

"I've just finished doing the research for a book entitled, *How to Break 90—Consistently!*"

"You? You're an author?"

"I am."

He shook his head. "That's great—for you. But I've seen too many of these golf books, you know, by all the big-name pros. The trouble with those books is that they're designed to help a guy increase his drives from two hundred and forty yards to two seventy-five and to explode from a sand trap to within two feet of the pin. Me? I just want to be able to keep the ball in the fairway and get *out* of a trap. Period."

"Exactly. And that's why I didn't go to any of the big-name pros. Because you're right: Most of their advice is directed at the golfer who already has a pretty good idea of the basics of the game. I went to the club professionals, the guys who deal with duffers, or high-handicap golfers, every day of their working lives. Their advice is what this book is all about."

"Well, I'll certainly buy a copy. Is that what you meant by helping me?" He sounded dubious.

"Not really. You see, I think we both need each other. You need help with your game, and I need a guinea pig."

"A guinea pig?"

"Yes. I have to find out whether all that advice and all those suggestions I got from the pros really work. Do you want to try it?"

"How much time do I have to spend at it?"

"Are you willing to devote twenty to thirty minutes a day, plus either one round of golf or a long session on the practice tee once a week?"

"That's all? How long will the whole thing take?"

"Harvey, if it works, I'll take a week off in October of this year, and we'll go down to Pinehurst. If you can break ninety on the Number Two Course, then I'll know that this book can help *anybody.*"

"It's a deal. But . . . but . . . the Number Two Course at Pinehurst. Isn't that where they play the World Open?"

"That's the one."

"Jesus! I'll never break ninety there."

"That's what I want to find out. That's what a guinea pig means. Is it a deal?"

"It's a deal." He grinned. "You don't know what you're letting yourself in for."

"One thing is all important: You have to follow my advice faithfully, do what I tell you, practice the way I tell you to. What I'll be passing along to you is the consensus of opinions of all the professionals I've talked to about every conceivable part of the game. In a way, you'll be getting the advice of pros from some of the most exclusive country clubs in the area. Will you do it?"

"Yes, I'll do it. When do we start?"

"Right now. Each week we'll meet here and either practice or play. Each time, I'll give you the basics of one more facet of the game. As we play, I'll try to point out some of the ways of playing smart golf. It's going to be up to you to practice those basics until the following Monday. OK?"

"OK."

"Then let's go back to the practice tee. From what I've seen today, there's a hell of a lot to be done."

He groaned. "This sounds like work."

I stopped and looked at him. "Harvey, golf is a damn hard game to play well. You take the average guy off the street who's never bowled before and put him on a bowling alley, and there's a possibility—remote, I grant you, but still a possibility—that he'll roll a two hundred game.

"But you take that same average guy who's never played golf before and put him on a golf course, and there is absolutely *no way* that he'll break a hundred and fifty—if he counts every stroke from tee to cup."

Harvey cocked his head. "I never thought of it that way, but I suppose you're right."

"I told you twenty to thirty minutes every day. That's not so much work, is it?"

"No, it isn't. But why every day?"

"Because it's not only a matter of practicing golf, but of thinking golf, keeping it in your mind. You have to start forming mental pictures of your swing, of how to hit various shots. Most people play once a week, and the thought of golf never crosses their minds in between outings. I once played with a guy who would get to the fifth or sixth hole before he seemed to know he was even out on the course. If you come here with your mind blank, naturally it's going to take you a while to get warmed up, to get yourself to start thinking about your game, in short, to concentrate on golf. But if you've been thinking about it all week, it's no problem."

"I see."

"Now let's get back and get to work."

"What exactly are we going to do?"

"Did you see *The Exorcist?*"

"Yes."

"Well, let's just say that there are quite a few aspects of your game that have to be exorcised."

He grinned. "And I'll feel better afterward?"

"Remember how you felt when you started throwing clubs?"

"Damn right!"

"Believe me, you won't feel any worse."

2

The Grip

Imagine that you're holding a bird. . . .

When I told Harvey that we were going to start with the grip, he looked pained. Obviously, he considered it a waste of time.

"What difference does it make how I hold the club?" he said impatiently. "Let's get on to the important part, the swing, so I can really start whacking the ball."

Harvey's reaction was like that of a lot of other golfers who also have never broken 90. They think the grip is unimportant, almost boring, compared to the dramatic intricacies of the swing itself.

I explained to him that every single one of the club professionals I had consulted considered a good grip to be a vital ingredient in fashioning an acceptable golf game. In fact, many of them cited their club members' refusal to take the matter of grip seriously, or to correct a poor grip, as one of the important contributing factors to their continued high handicaps.*

The familiar Ben Franklin observation goes:

> A little neglect may breed great mischief.
> For want of a nail the shoe was lost,
> For want of a shoe the horse was lost,
> For want of a horse the rider was lost,
> For want of a rider the battle was lost,
> For want of a battle the kingdom was lost,
> Thus, for want of a nail a kingdom was lost.

Similarly, you might also say, "For want of a good grip, a golf game was lost." For, in this case, a little neglect can indeed breed great mischief. If the grip is wrong, nothing you can do will compensate for it. For the grip determines at what angle the clubhead meets the ball, and if the clubface alignment at the moment of impact is out of whack, a score of 89 will be forever out of reach.

Although the consensus opinion is that how you hold the club may well determine how you play the game, the reason this is true has not always been made clear. One way to explain it might be to think of the children's game of "crack-the-whip," in which a long line of boys and girls joins hands in a chain, picks up some speed on skates, and the leader then stops suddenly and spins the long line in a circle. The boy or girl at the end of the line is soon being propelled at very great speed.

The same principle applies to a golf swing—with the

---

* In italics throughout this book I have included some verbatim tips from the professionals I talked to on how to grip the club properly, the swing, and other elements of the game.

clubhead being the end of the chain. The player's only contact with the club is through his hands. With a poor grip, a golfer can neither control the club at the top of his swing, nor generate maximum power on the downswing.

TIPS ON GRIP from Tom Cochan, Professional, Round Hill Country Club, Greenwich, Connecticut

I can't overemphasize the importance of the grip. It determines everything. You can have a perfect swing, but if you have a bad grip, you will not play good golf.

In my opinion, the most important thing in the grip is to make sure that the hands are placed on the club so that they are exactly lined up with the clubhead at rest on the ground. To achieve this, I tell my students to grip the shaft right up next to the clubhead. When their hands and the clubhead are only an inch or two apart, they can see clearly when the two are lined up properly. Then all they have to do is to slide their hands back along the shaft without turning the club—and their hands will automatically be in the right position. The hands have to work as one, and the only way this is possible is if the clubhead and the right and left hands are facing the identical angle and direction.

Try and remember the look of people's hands as they walk down the street. You'll notice that the fingers are not straight and tense, but naturally relaxed and slightly curled. The hands have to feel just as natural and relaxed when they grip the club. Because when they hit the ball, the hands tend to return to their natural, comfortable position.

How hard should one grip the club? I have found that a great many people hold the club much too tightly, perhaps because of our natural instinct to hit everything with our hands. They seem to be under the impression that the tighter they hold the club, the farther they're going to hit the ball. Which is dead wrong! I tell my beginners to hold the golf club with exactly the same pressure they would use if they

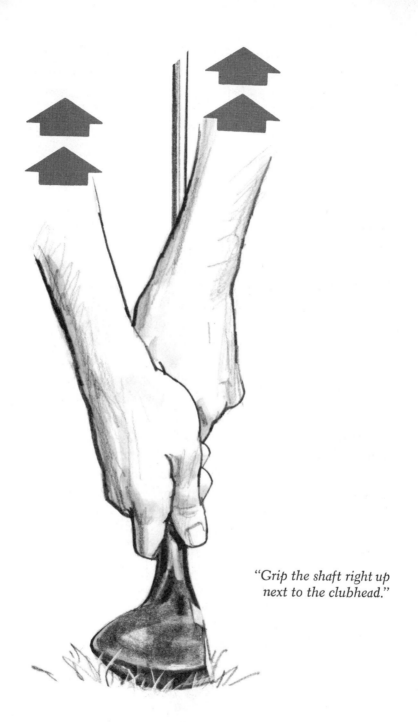

"Grip the shaft right up next to the clubhead."

*were holding a bird just hard enough to keep its wings against
its body. You can't squeeze it—either the bird or the club.
And if your grip is too tight, two things will probably happen
on your backswing: (1) Your left arm will bend badly, and
(2) you won't be able to cock your wrists. So hold the club
gently—like a bird!*

At the very beginning I said to Harvey, "One of the
things I learned from the club pros is that there is no single
and absolute way to hold the club. You, Harvey, have to find
the right grip for you, one that will best enable you to bring
the clubhead all the way through the backswing and downswing back to the same position at the instant you hit the ball
as the clubhead was when you were addressing the ball.

"There seem to be two key ingredients whatever grip you
decide upon," I told him. "It should feel comfortable for you,
and it should give you the best control of the club."

Comfort is all important. If you buy a pair of shoes that
pinch, whenever you walk on them you are aware of that
discomfort. It drives everything else from your mind. There
is a classic story about a man with a terrific headache who
bashed his finger accidentally with a hammer. Later, he was
heard to say, "You know, for about thirty seconds there, I
forgot all about my headache."

It's the same with a grip that feels uncomfortable. No
matter what may be wrong with your swing, no matter how
many things you're trying to remember, no matter how hard
you're trying to *concentrate, concentrate,* all you'll be able to
think of is that damn grip. So, don't worry if your grip has
the approval of Johnny Miller, or whether it's been officially
sanctioned by the PGA. The main thing is: Does it feel good
to you?

TIPS ON GRIP from Walt Ronan, Professional, Bedford
Golf & Tennis Club, Bedford Village, New York

*For me, the most important element in the grip is mak-
ing sure that the palms of both hands are as close together
as possible. When I teach a beginner about the grip, I ask
him to grasp the end of the club with his left hand and pass
it to me. Then I try to pull the club away from him, telling
him to resist. He then can feel the pressure against the last
three fingers of his left hand. That's the same pressure he
should feel at the top of his backswing.*

*Then I tell him to let the clubhead rest naturally on the
ground, still holding the shaft with the left hand alone. Now
he should put his right hand on the club so that the cup of
this hand lies on top of the "V" formed by the thumb and
forefinger of the left hand. The palms should be close together, hands relaxed, with the left thumb completely covered by the right hand. At that point, he should feel that his
hands have been glued together to form one hand.*

The second key ingredient for an effective grip is to gain
complete control of the clubhead. Although shoulder turn,
hip turn, weight transfer, and all the other elements of the
swing are important, remember that it is the hands that di-
rect the clubhead to the ball. It is the hands that will determine the direction of the ball. When you get a grip you
like, wiggle the clubhead back and forth. Do you feel that
your hands are in complete control of the clubhead? Take
a few practice swings. Can you feel your hands "working"?
Does the club feel alive in your hands, or is it just a dead
weight? Only *you* can answer such questions.

Harvey and I experimented with several different grips.
His hands were fairly large and quite strong, so the baseball
grip, or ten fingers on the club, did not feel right to him at all.

25

(It's much more suited to small-handed people.) The inter-locking grip was much too radical and uncomfortable for him, and he just laughed when we tried the cross-handed grip. So, we turned to the grip that is used by the overwhelming majority of golfers—the Vardon, or overlapping, grip, in which the pinky of the right hand overlaps the first and second fingers of the left hand.

I'll describe how to get this grip, just as I did to Harvey.

1. Take out your driver and hold it loosely with your left hand in a tee-off position.

2. Place your right hand a bit down the shaft and lift the club until it is sticking out in front of you. Let go with your left hand.

3. Place the club in the left hand so that the end of the shaft is pressed against the muscular pad on the inside of the palm. Close the fingers, then the thumb. The club should now be positioned correctly.

4. Place the top three fingers around the club as close to the left hand as possible and in such a way that the pinky lies between and on top of the first and second fingers of the left hand. Fold the right hand over on top of the left thumb so that no space is visible in between. The more space the hands take up, the more difficult it is for them to act as a unit. The more snugly they fit together, the more control and power they can generate.

5. Keep adjusting the fingers of the right hand slightly until the grip feels perfectly comfortable. It is important that both hands feel as one. They should not feel like individual units but as one "welded" unit with the power equally distributed throughout.

6. Grasp the club gently but firmly enough so that you will not lose your grip on it when you swing. But don't imag-

ine that you're choking a snake. Your grip will automatically tighten when you begin your downswing.

7. Make sure that the "Vs" formed by joining the fingers and thumbs of both hands are pointing toward the right side of the head. When the right hand is turned over too far, the clubhead will open at impact and the ball will slice. If it is not turned over far enough, that is, does not fit snugly against the left, the clubhead will close at impact and a hook will result.

8. Wiggle the clubhead. Does one hand feel stronger than the other? It shouldn't. Open the tops of your hands a little. You should be able to see that the club is being held by the last three fingers of the left hand and the middle two of the right.

9. Take a couple of slow practice swings, concentrating on the "feel" of your hands. Are there certain points in your swing when your grip feels uncomfortable, or when your hands tend to lose their grip? See if you can correct this by adjustment until you feel you have complete control of the club throughout.

10. Once you know your grip is right for you, study it closely and see exactly how you are holding the club. It is absolutely essential that you use the same grip every time. And once you have mastered it, you can forget about it.

Harvey and I worked a while, making minor adjustments in this grip, until he understood how it functioned and why. After he had taken a number of practice swings, I asked him how his new grip felt.

"Pretty good," he admitted. "It felt kind of funny at first, you know, sort of strange and unnatural. But now when I swing, I find it's the first time I've been able to take a full swing without letting go of the club a little."

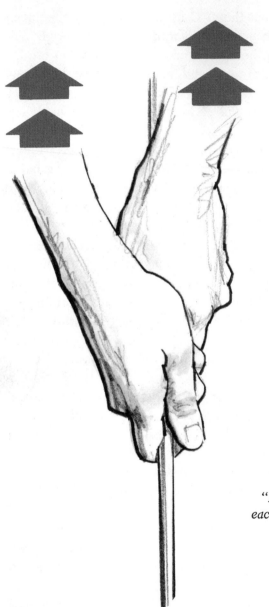

"Make sure the 'Vs' of each hand are lined up."

"Do your hands feel as one unit?"

"They do now. They didn't before."

"It felt unnatural to you because you've always held the club with your hands turned way around clockwise."

"What's wrong with that?"

"For one thing, you shouldn't see all the knuckles on your left hand. You know, Harvey, just from your old grip I can make a good guess as to your golf history. I'll bet that you never played before World War II. Then, when you started, I doubt if you ever took any lessons from a pro; you probably picked up all your information from a book on golf."

"Right on the nail." He looked surprised. "How did you figure that out?"

"For a period there in the late forties and early fifties, many people thought that a slight hook was the perfect shot. The theory sprung up that to achieve that ideal hook, you had to turn your hands to the right so that you could pronate, or roll your hands, at impact. But it turned out that it was a lot harder to do than it sounded. Now the theory is a bit different."

"Different from what you've shown me?"

"Yes. The grip you have now will take the clubhead back straight and return it the way it was when you started. With your old grip, you had to compensate to achieve that same effect."

"But don't you have to snap your wrists?"

"Yes. But you don't have to *think* about snapping them, or to try to do it. If your swing is right and you get in the proper hitting position and start your downswing, your hands and wrists will take over by instinct."

I asked him to practice swinging the club with this grip as often as possible. "You might even want to take a club into the office with you. And, whenever you get a break, or before and after lunch, pick up the club and establish this grip. Not only your mind but your hands have to learn it so thoroughly that it will become instinctive whenever you pick up a club. Your grip must never change once you've got it right—except, perhaps, for putting. But you'll use that same grip for every other shot, so learn it well."

"That's a good idea. I'll do it."

Harvey had taken the first giant step.

TIPS ON GRIP from Vince Paccadolmi, Professional, Waccabuc Country Club, Waccabuc, New York

When I'm teaching the grip, I ask my students to hold their hands straight in front of them with all fingers touching. Then I ask them to bend the four fingers of each hand, keeping both thumbs straight, so that the fingertips are touching the palms. I ask them to study their hands in that position. They can see that with each hand a "V" has been formed between the thumb and the base of the forefinger.

I do it that way because, for me, the most important part of the grip is insuring that the "Vs" of each hand are lined up, one on top of the other. If the right hand is turned too far clockwise, or the left hand too far counterclockwise, those "Vs" will not be in line. And I don't care what kind of grip you have, the Vardon, or the interlocking, or ten fingers on the club, what is important is that those "Vs" be in perfect alignment.

When they are, then your hands can work as a team. You won't end up with, say, left hand weak and right hand strong, which causes one hand to fight the other. The main purpose of a good grip is to enable you to square the clubface at the moment of impact. Just remember, "Vs" for Victory.

3

The Stance

Imagine you're a commuter and you've just come home from work. . . .

"A stance is like a glove," I said to Harvey. "It has to fit the person. In your case, you've got the wrong size."

"What's wrong with my stance?" He was positively indignant.

"You're standing too far away from the ball, and your feet are too far apart."

"But that's the way I get my distance," he protested.

"You think so? Study any of the touring pros. See how close they stand to the ball, and they certainly get distance."

"But I'm not built like Johnny Miller."

"It doesn't make any difference how you're built. The fact is that when you stand too far from the ball, your weight

31

is bound to be on your toes, and that's not where it's supposed to be."

"How do I know the right place to stand?"

I told Harvey to take a stance with his feet about shoulder-width apart, knees barely flexed, and the weight on the balls of his feet.

"You should feel comfortable and relaxed. Do you?"

When he nodded, I put a driver in his left hand and told him to let the clubhead fall naturally to the ground. When he did that, I moved the clubhead so that it was lined up just inside his left foot.

"That's approximately how far away you should be from the ball," I told him.

"My God!" he said shaking his head. "That's much too close. I'll never even hit the ball."

"You'll hit it," I reassured him. "It's just that your swing won't be so flat any more."

TIPS ON STANCE from Robert Cloughan, Professional, Ridgewood Country Club, Danbury, Connecticut

I ask a golfer to take a practice swing and try to hit the ground hard enough to make a mark. Then I measure the distance between the mark and the end of his toes. That's where he should be standing when there's a ball there. Why? Usually, in a practice swing, a person will swing the club more slowly, more naturally. It's when he's addressing the ball that he has a tendency to get into an unnatural stance, to strain, to contort himself.

And when I tell someone to move closer to the ball, he doesn't think he can hit it from that spot. But after he has hit a few, I say to him, "Look at the balance you have now. You're not falling forward after you hit the ball. Your weight is on your left foot at the end of your swing, where it's supposed to be."

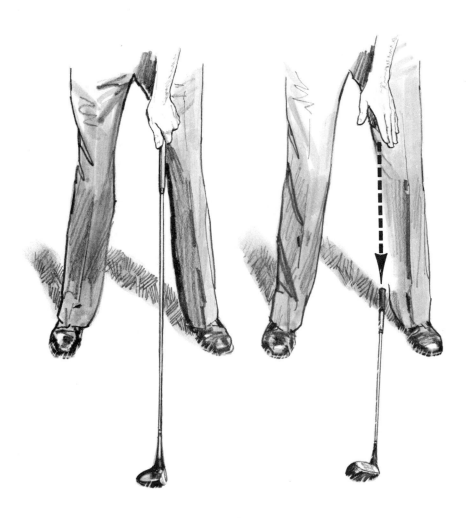

*"That's approximately how far away
you should be from the ball."*

I told him to try to get the distance he was standing away from the ball in his mind's eye so that he would automatically stand in the same spot every time.

"If you want to check yourself as to whether you're at the right distance, there's a simple way. Just let the club fall to the ground between your legs. You can see that the spot where the grip starts on the club is lying next to your left heel. Keep practicing that every chance you get, and pretty soon you won't have to think about it. It will be done naturally. Of course, the shorter the club, the closer you'll have to stand to the ball and the narrower your stance will become. But if you can master the position with the driver, everything else will fall into place."

"But I don't always play it off the left foot, do I?"

"No. With each higher club you'll play the ball more to the right. The driver is almost off the left foot, while the nine-iron is almost off the right. Your fairway irons, the four and the five, should be played about in the middle, equidistant from each foot."

"It still feels funny to be so close to the ball."

"OK. Move back to your old stance." When he did, I asked, "Now what have you changed when you moved back?"

"I don't know."

"Look down at your feet."

"They're much wider apart," he said, surprised.

"That's right. When you stand too far from the ball, you instinctively widen your stance for better balance. And you bend your knees too much, like you're doing, which stops you from making a proper turn. Also look at your hands. When you stand too far away, there's a strong tendency to grip the club too tightly. If you were holding a bird, you would have killed it by now. Tell me, does that stance feel comfortable?"

"Well, I'm used to it. I guess it does."

"Then stand that way for awhile without moving."

The seconds passed. After about 30 of them, Harvey began to fidget. "My legs are beginning to hurt," he complained.

"Hold it a little longer."

After a minute, beads of sweat popped out on his forehead. "Now my back and arms ache too," he said.

"OK. You can relax. I just wanted you to realize how unnatural your old stance was. You were all tense and straining. But if you stand the way I showed you, you can hold the position for an hour because you're comfortable and relaxed to begin with."

He took the new stance once more, but this time his knees were locked stiff. I told him to relax them slightly.

"Think of other sports, Harvey. Take a shortstop waiting for the ball to be hit in his direction, or a tennis player about to receive a serve, and their knees are invariably bent, with the weight on the balls of their feet, so that they are able to move easily in any direction. It's the same with golf. You have to move into the shot—and you can't do it stiff-legged."

"I see."

"OK. I've told you how to stand, but not why."

I then explained to Harvey that the whole purpose of a good stance was to position yourself in the right line. Many golfers, even though they make good contact with the ball, end up in the woods simply because they were aiming in that direction. So it is all important that your feet are positioned in such a way that they are exactly parallel to the target.

"How often have you heard a golfer say, 'I hit that good, but it hooked into the rough?' Well, I've played with enough golfers to know that very often the ball didn't hook at all; it went straight as an arrow. The trouble was that the guy was simply aiming to the left."

35

"Is the club pointing exactly at the target?"

TIPS ON STANCE from Tom Murphy, Professional, Sleepy Hollow Country Club, Tarrytown, New York

The most common fault I've found with poor golfers is that they simply do not line up properly—they don't aim in the right direction. I would say that 95 percent of the duffers I know aim too far to the right. They do this because basically they're afraid of a slice, and they figure if they close the face of the club and swing from the inside out, they'll hook —so they aim right. What usually happens is that they end up looping their swing and blocking any hip turn—and the ball goes to the right and continues to the right.

I think you should stand as close to the ball as possible. That way you'll be forced into a more upright swing. With regard to knee flex, I've found that if you do stand close to the ball, there will be very little bend in the knees, with the exception of tall players. The weight should be on the balls of your feet, the same way it would be if you started to touch your toes.

There were two pieces of advice the pros gave me to help golfers line up correctly, and I passed them along to Harvey.

"The first thing is to approach your ball from directly behind it, not from the side, looking from it to the target on a straight line. Next, select the spot where you want the ball to go. Then, after you've made your club selection, while standing behind the ball and always looking at the target, take your stance and check your feet alignment closely.

"The second suggestion was to lay your club on the ground next to your toes. Is the club pointing exactly at the target? Or is it to the right? Or to the left? This is very important, Harvey. The two basic elements of golf are direction and distance. It doesn't make a damn bit of difference how far you hit the ball if you're aiming in the wrong direction. And your stance largely determines that. A mental lapse in checking your direction will cost you strokes every time. Playing good golf is the elimination of such mental lapses. Do you get all this, Harvey?"

"Sure," he said quickly, but I didn't quite believe him.

"Look Harvey, one of the pros, Vince Paccadolmi, told me a story about communication in golf. A new member of his club, a young lawyer, came to him for some lessons. As Vince was giving him the first lesson, he became aware that the guy was not getting the message but was too proud to admit it. So Vince went into some real technical golf jargon, and the guy nodded in understanding. So Vince said to him, 'Tommy, you didn't understand a word I said, and it's important that you do. If I went to your law office with a problem and you began to give me this business of section five, paragraph two, and the Party of the First Part, I would stop you and ask you to put it in language that I understood. I gave you that golf gobbledegook on purpose to make you realize that if you don't understand what I'm talking about, you have to ask me to spell it out in a way that you *can* understand.' "

"Do you get the point, Harvey?"

He looked sheepish. "OK. What's bothering me is that I remember hearing that your weight should be on your heels."

"That's a good point. I think the reason that has been stated is to make sure that a golfer does not have his weight on his toes. But it's a matter of balance, Harvey. Stand there with all your weight on your heels. Go ahead. Put all your weight back on your heels. Don't you feel that if someone pushed you softly, you would fall backwards? That's because you're not in a balanced position. Comfort, balance, and alignment are the important elements in a stance."

"Doesn't a wider stance let you hit the ball further?"

"No, and I'll show you why. Take a real wide stance.

Now turn your hips as much as you can. You can't turn them very far, can you? Now put your feet close together and turn your hips. See how easily they pivot? All of which means that if you have a very wide stance, you'll probably hit the ball mostly with your hands and arms—and you can't get any real distance that way."

"Do all the pros agree with this method?"

"There are hundreds of different theories on every facet of the golf swing, Harvey. What I'm giving you is the consensus opinion. Also, I've tried to make it as simple as possible. Golf is a tough enough game without cluttering your mind with methods and theories. If your grip and stance are basically sound, you'll be all right."

He nodded. "I think I've got it now. What's next?"

"Something that will make you happy."

"What?"

"We go on to the swing itself."

TIPS ON STANCE from Vince Paccadolmi, Professional, Waccabuc Country Club, Waccabuc, New York

Your stance gives you two things, direction and balance. In terms of the width of your feet, the old advice used to be that the insides of your feet should be no further apart than the width of your shoulders. But some of us club pros think that's too rigid an attitude. A very tall person will need a wider stance. Because he makes a bigger arc, he needs a little more base for his swing to maintain his balance.

The weight should not be on the heels, but toward the back of the feet. If a person is on his toes, chances are good that he's standing too far from the ball. And if he is, he'll probably pick up the club with an outside-in swing, not make a good shoulder turn—and end up with a banana ball.

As far as flexing the knees, I handle that situation this way. A lot of my club members are commuters, so I say to

them: *Imagine that you've just gotten home from work. You're going to have a drink with your wife and the evening paper is on the table by your chair. She's fixing you a drink. You're glancing at the headlines and you reach down to hitch up your pants prior to sitting down, flexing your knees just a bit and—that's the way your stance should be. You don't want them bent too much, or locked in place, just relaxed enough so that you can make a proper turn.*

4

The Swing: Part I

*To get an elementary grasp of the game of golf, a
human must learn, by endless practice, a continuous
and subtle series of highly unnatural movements,
involving about 64 muscles, that result in a seemingly
"natural" swing, taking all of two seconds to begin and
end.*

—Alistair Cooke

I told Harvey to forget every piece of advice he had ever
heard about such things as "sliding one's hips," or swinging
"inside out," or "keeping one's head down," or "rolling one's
wrists." A person, I pointed out, can really remember one
thing at a time, and when you're standing in front of a golf
ball, the last thing you want is to have a thousand pieces of
advice running around in your head like so many frantic
bats. Beside, there was only one thing I wanted him to think
about when he began to swing a golf club.

"Assuming grip and stance are correct," I said slowly,
"a good golf shot occurs only when the clubhead at impact
moves exactly along the target line and is squarely lined up

"Picture yourself standing on one track of a railroad preparing to hit a ball that is teed up on the other track."

with the target. There is a big difference between swinging the clubhead and hitting with it."

"All right, you asked me to level. I really don't know what you mean by that."

"OK. I'll try and make it graphically clear. Imagine that I have a string with a rock tied to the end of it. I hold the string over the spot where you would normally address the ball. If I pull the rock straight back and release it, it will travel back along the exact same line, just like a pendulum. If I pull it back at an angle, it will also travel back along that same line and pass over the impact point at an angle. The same way, if your clubhead goes back at an angle, it will probably meet the ball at an angle—and cause it to hook, slice, pull, or push. Therefore, the most important thing to be aware of is bringing the clubhead straight back."

"But I've been doing that, haven't I?"

"You wouldn't have been slicing so badly if you had. What you've been doing is consciously trying to bring the club back on the inside, and this has caused you to loop at the top so that your downswing was then traveling at an angle—from outside in— and you ended up with a slice."

I explained to him that one of the most vivid methods I had found to insure that the clubhead goes back straight was devised by the great British teacher, John Jacobs, and was used by one of the pros I talked to, Tom Murphy at Sleepy Hollow Country Club. It was the so-called "railroad-track" approach. "Picture yourself standing on one track of a railroad preparing to hit a ball that is teed up on the other track. This should give you the mental image of proper alignment, as well as stressing the necessity of bringing the clubhead back along the track, not across it in either direction."

What I did with Harvey was to lay two clubs on the ground simulating railroad tracks. Then I had him practice his backswing between the two clubs as long as possible.

43

After a while he said, "It feels strange, as though I'm taking it back far away from me."

"That's because you're so used to that inside backswing. But remember the pendulum, Harvey. Bringing the clubhead back on a straight line is the first important ingredient to a good swing."

DON'T SWING "INSIDE OUT"

The most misused phrase in golf today is "swinging inside out." That's the worst thing you can dwell on—to try consciously to swing from the inside out. When you do, you will unconsciously develop a loop in your swing—and a slice. If you take the clubhead back straight and make a proper shoulder turn, you will automatically swing from the inside out without even thinking about it.
—Tom Cochan, Round Hill Country Club

Harvey swung a few more times, and I noticed something else he was doing.

"You're picking the clubhead up, Harvey. When you do that, it forces you to break your wrists too soon. Bring the clubhead back as close to the ground as you can. Arnold Palmer says that the first twelve inches of the backswing are the most important. He says that probably because in that short distance you have to start the direction of the swing, you establish the tempo of your swing, and you have to keep the clubhead low to the ground. Remember, the way you bring the clubhead back is usually the way you'll bring it down again. If you lift the clubhead, chances are you'll smash down at the ball when you try to hit it."

He took a few practice swings, then held his backswing at the top and looked at it. His left arm was slightly bent, and instinctively he straightened it. I smiled, because a straight left arm seems to be one of the sacred cows of a golf swing. Then I told him what Bob Cloughan of Ridgewood Country Club had told me about it. Said Cloughan: "I feel there's a misconception about the absolute necessity of keeping your left arm rigidly straight on the backswing. If your hands are relaxed, the left arm will automatically straighten at the moment of impact—and that's when it counts."

I felt it was now time to go on to the second vital ingredient in a good golf swing, a proper shoulder turn, and I decided to illustrate it with a technique used by Walt Ronan of Bedford Golf and Tennis Club. I asked Harvey to put the driver behind his back and to hold it there by the crooks of his two elbows. Then I asked him to make a backswing and hold it. He did. The end of the club was now pointing directly out in front of him.

"It shouldn't be there," I told him. "You've made the lateral turn but not the up-and-down turn. The end of the club should be pointing right down at the ball."

He adjusted his shoulders so that it was.

I nodded. "That's the way a shoulder turn should feel."

"One thing I know," he said. "I certainly haven't been doing *that* before. This is a completely new feeling."

"No, you haven't. You've been swinging mostly with your hands and arms. But when you turn your shoulder like you're doing now, you'll be able to generate much more power."

I asked him to take a practice swing, trying to make a proper shoulder turn, and hold it at the top. He did, and I took the club and put it behind his back again, held by his elbows.

"You see? The end of the club is still not pointing down at the ground."

Once again he adjusted his shoulder correctly.

45

"Now look down at your left leg. See how much the knee is bent in toward the right? That will happen every time you make a good shoulder turn. If it isn't bent that way, you haven't turned in the right direction."

FORMING A TRIANGLE

I ask my students to think of the point of each shoulder and the two hands gripped together as three points that form a triangle. When the backswing is started, the important thing is that the triangle moves, not just the hands. The fault most duffers make on the backswing is letting the hands and wrists travel faster than the body. When the hands and wrists start to take control of the club, the body stops turning. The longer you can keep the triangle going, the more you're going to swing *the clubhead, rather than hitting with it.*

—Tom Murphy, Sleepy Hollow Country Club

Harvey kept practicing the shoulder turn, but I could see that he hadn't quite got the feel of it, for he still looked awkward and uncomfortable.

"Stop for a minute, Harvey, and address the ball. Let's try another way of helping you get the picture. Imagine if you can that you have no arms. The club—a much longer version —is attached to your left shoulder. You have to make a backswing without using your arms because you have none. But the end of the club is a part of your body and is attached at the left shoulder. See if you can do it."

He took the club back slowly, and because he obviously had gotten the mental picture of it being attached to his left shoulder, the only way he could do it was to make a full shoulder turn.

"The club—a much longer version—is attached to your left shoulder. You have to make a backswing without using your arms. . . ."

"That's perfect," I told him.

"I see," he said smiling. "I think I've got it now."

"You probably haven't got it yet. It will take time and practice, but at least you've got the picture. One of the pros told me that the shoulder turn was probably the hardest thing to learn in a golf swing, because it's not natural. Human instinct is to *hit* a ball. Nobody has to be taught that. What people have to learn is to overcome their natural instinct in the *way* they hit a ball.

"The average person who has never played golf will instinctively do one thing when you hand him a club and tell him to hit a golf ball. He will lift up the clubhead, bring it high over his head, and strike down at the ball, using only his hands and arms. But the whole purpose of a golf swing is to return the clubhead at maximum speed to the same position it was when you addressed the ball—and it's impossible to do that using only your hands and arms. There's just too much weight at the end of a forty-three-inch club to be able to control it with hands and arms alone. The key has to be in the shoulder, which should be thought of as the hinge of the swing."

"And my hinge was rusty?" he chuckled.

"Your hinge was nonexistent, as it is with most high-handicap golfers. Again, it's because it's not an instinctive thing; it has to be learned and mastered. Most poor golfers do not make a shoulder turn, and the results are evident on any golf course: A guy stands over a ball and lifts the club with his hands and his arms. But because he doesn't make a shoulder turn, he ends up swinging and falling back from the ball. He has no balance when he swings that way. Fire and fall back, one pro calls it."

"That's me," Harvey said ruefully.

"That *was* you," I told him, "if you really want to work at it and concentrate."

DON'T FORGET THAT SHOULDER TURN

The shoulder turn is by far the most important part of a golf swing. I don't know a single good golfer who does not make a proper shoulder turn. I would go as far as to say that without a good turn, you will never play good golf. One way to help you make that turn is to take back the clubhead low to the ground for as long as you can. This will propel you into a shoulder turn as the clubhead moves back.

To enable my golfers to get a mental picture of a shoulder turn, I ask them to hold the shaft of the club parallel to the ground with the clubhead pointing toward the target. Hold the club in the middle with the hands about a foot apart. Then take a backswing. With the hands held apart, the shoulder has to turn. This is not only a good warm-up device, but it gives people the feel of a proper shoulder turn. Incidentally, failure to make a shoulder turn is one of the main reasons people bend their left arm so badly.

—Tom Cochan, Round Hill Country Club

"I said I would, and I meant it."

"OK, I'm not going to give you any more today. You have enough to think about and work on. Why don't you get a bucket of balls and hit a few?"

For the next half hour I watched Harvey hit some balls, occasionally making a suggestion or a correction. He was still doing a lot of things wrong, but he was also doing some things right which he hadn't been doing before. His grip looked good—the "Vs" were lined up—and he held the club loosely. He was standing closer to the ball and his stance was narrower. His shoulder turn was not full yet, but there was a definite turn.

At first, he began to top a lot of shots, and I suggested he use a 3-wood instead of a driver.

"All of the pros I talked to felt that many people

should not be using a driver off the tee, simply because it is harder to hit than a three-wood. The first thing you have to do off the tee, Harvey, is to get the ball airborne. The three-wood has a shorter shaft, it's more lofted, it has a smaller head—all of which should give you confidence in your ability to get the ball in the air. Forget about distance. So you're ten or fifteen yards shorter with a three-wood than a driver, but you'll hit the three-wood well many more times—and that's what really matters. Remember, always select the club that gives you the most room for error."

He went to his 3-wood, and his shots improved immediately.

USE THE CLUB THAT'S EASY TO HIT

Players should use lofted clubs whenever they can. They'll play better. That fact is reflected in the sale of golf equipment in recent years. Today, there are many sets being sold with irons 4 through 9 plus the sand wedge, and woods 3, 4, 6, and 7. Your high-handicap golfer can hit a 6- or 7-wood, with its little head and high-lofted face, when there's no way he can hit a 2- or 3-iron. That's because most golfers hit down at the ball. If they hit down with a 2-iron, they'll dribble it along the ground. But if they hit down with a 6-wood, the ball will go up. And, after all, the name of the game is confidence.
—Tom Murphy, Sleepy Hollow Country Club

At one point, he complained that he was hitting a lot of shots off the heel of the club.

"That's because you occasionally revert to the old flat swing of yours where you're reaching for the ball. Naturally, you're going to hit it on the heel of the club. Just keep remembering the railroad tracks and bring the clubhead straight back and up."

He hit one good shot, then hit behind the ball and took a divot. He asked me why he had done that.

"It looked to me like you picked up the clubhead and tried to hit down on it too hard with your hands and arms. Try to get the feeling that the clubhead is moving through the ball, not at it."

Watching him hit the practice balls, I had to admit that his swing looked better, smoother, more compact. He still had a slice, but it was not of the roundhouse variety. Apparently, there was still a slight loop in his swing. And when he made good contact, the ball was going out a considerable distance.

"I've still got a slice," he said accusingly.

"Don't worry about it now. Concentrate on the things I told you—the railroad tracks, proper grip, a comfortable stance close to the ball, not swinging too hard, bringing the clubhead back low. One more thing you might try is picking out a target to aim at, a tree or a mound. That way you'll be able to find out if you're lining up properly."

He hit two more shots, and the ball sliced badly each time. "Wow! That looks like the old me."

I handed Harvey a balled-up handkerchief. "Put this under your right arm, in the armpit, and hold it there with your arm."

When he had done that, I asked him to take a practice swing. He did, and the handkerchief fluttered to the ground.

"When that happens, it means that you're going back to your old habit of consciously taking the clubhead back too far to the inside. Then you loop badly at the top, your right elbow flies out away from your body, and you slice. That's one of the hardest things you're going to have to do—forget all those bad habits. Just remember, if you take the clubhead straight back and bring it down the same way, and you keep that elbow in tight, the handkerchief won't fall out."

He tried it several times, and there was no handkerchief. "I'll be damned," he said. "It really works."

"I think you've had about enough for today. You've got a lot to remember."

"What about practicing?"

"Harvey, practice is the only way you're going to learn to forget your old ways and start mastering the new ones. But it depends on the *way* you practice. There's no point in practicing if you're practicing the wrong things. I'll outline the various practicing methods for you in detail. But for now, do you want to meet me here next week for another session?"

"You're damn right. For the first time, this damn game is beginning to make a little bit of sense to me."

"That reminds me of the man who fell off a skyscraper, and as he passed the twenty-seventh floor he was heard to say, 'So far, so good.'"

5

Tips from the Pros
on Practicing

*There is simply no substitute for practice, because
there is no shortcut to playing good golf.*

Practicing golf is to playing on a course what internship is
to private practice. A golfer can no more go from instruction
right out onto a golf course than can a second-year medical
student undertake an operation. There has to be a bridge between the two stages, and that bridge is simply *practice*.

All of the pros I talked with were definite about the
necessity of practice if you want to improve your game. One
went as far as to say that if you spent a total of twelve hours a
month on golf, at least six of them should be spent practicing.
But the average high-handicap golfer has neither the time nor
the desire to devote himself to that much work. Still, one

hour of the *right* kind of practice is worth six hours of aimless and compulsive driving contests. Harvey was willing to devote an hour a week to practice. Are you? If you are, here are some of the pros' suggestions on how to make your practice sessions really pay off. I'll give them to you just as I outlined them to Harvey.

The Practice Range. One of the advantages of playing on a course is that you have time between shots to think about what you're going to do when you reach the ball. You have time to analyze what you may have done wrong your last shot and to evaluate your present situation as far as position, distance to the target, wind conditions, placement of the pin, and club selection. You also have time to prepare yourself mentally before each shot, to go over in your mind the things you want to do to hit a good shot.

That's also the major *disadvantage* of a practice range, and it's a trap that all too many golfers have never gotten out of. For the temptation is enormous to just keep setting up ball after ball on a tee and letting fly. One ball after another, without pause, without thought.

But that needn't, and shouldn't, be the case. There is a way to make your time on a practice tee meaningful.

For one thing, leave your driver in the bag. Heresy? No. Common sense. Because it's so much easier to hit an 8- or 9-iron, that's the way you should start your practicing. Begin with your short irons—preferably off grass—then go on to your middle and long irons. When you do get to the woods, the more lofted ones should come first. The driver should be the very last club you pick up. With most golfers, it's the first—and often the only—club they use.

The second thing is, take it easy. You're not in a race against time. No one is going to give you a prize if you finish hitting your bucket of balls before anyone else. Put your head to work as well as your body. Imagine that you're out on a golf course. Each shot you hit at the range should be an imaginary shot out on that golf course and made with the same thought, deliberation, and concentration you would use if this shot determined the outcome of a two-dollar Nassau.

Take a couple of practice swings, loosen up. Then pick out a specific target out on the range, one of the markers perhaps. Tee your ball up and select the proper club for that distance. Again, do the same thing you would do if this were an actual shot on a course. Check your grip, your stance. Are you lined up correctly? When you swing, keep it on the slow side. That way, if you do mishit the ball, you'll have a better idea what you did wrong.

There, you've hit the ball, but you're about 20 yards short of your target. Take a slightly longer club and hit it again. Right distance, but you sliced it this time. Lay two clubs on the ground, about a foot apart, pointing toward the target and on either side of your ball. When you start your backswing, make sure that the clubhead bisects the area between the two clubs. If it crosses either club, you're not going back straight. Hit another one. Still slicing a bit? Check your grip. Are the "Vs" lined up?

Incidentally, don't rely on the yard markers at most ranges. They have probably been designed more for flattery than for accuracy. So when you hit a good shot and your ball snuggles up to the 250-yard marker, don't have dreams of glory. Don't immediately translate that accomplishment out onto the course and think that now you can carry that 235-yard par-three over water. You've probably hit the ball 210 or 220 yards at most. Be content with that distance. On a course, if you can do that every time and keep it in the fairway, you'll be in great shape.

THINK ON THE PRACTICE TEE

After a person has some instruction, he should go to the practice range as soon as possible. It's a matter of logic. Say you get a bad burn and go to the doctor for help. He gives you a certain salve and tells you to put it on your hand every day. But you forget to do it. The next week you go back to the doctor and your hand is no better; in fact, it's worse.

It's the same with practicing. If you take a lesson on Saturday, do nothing connected with golf all week, and come out and play the following Saturday, you'll be worse than you were before. That's because you'll be thinking about that lesson on the golf course, when you should have thought about it on the practice tee. You tell your kids to do their homework or they won't learn what they're being taught in school. Well, this is your homework, and if you don't do it you'll never play decent golf.

I have a friend who owns a meat market. One day I was in his market and asked him how to slice a leg of lamb properly. He was nice enough to show me. But about six weeks later, when we had lamb for dinner, I still hacked it up. I had forgotten everything he had shown me. I hadn't practiced it once. You see, there is simply no substitute for practice, because there is no shortcut to playing good golf.

—Robert Cloughan, Ridgewood Country Club

When you're hitting balls, don't try to remember too many things you're supposed to be doing—or not doing. For about ten or twelve swings, concentrate on doing one thing correctly until it's firmly in your mind. Then go on to the next thing. Trying to remember bits of advice simultaneously will only confuse you. And you don't even have to be on a practice range. Two or three times a day, swing a club back and forth. What you're trying to do is keep the swing memory alive.

It also helps to practice downwind, against the wind, and in a crosswind. The wind may affect your ball differently than it does someone else's. How much distance is cut from your 5-iron, say, when you hit it into the wind? How much does your 8-iron drift when a crosswind catches it? These are things you can learn precisely on a practice range. If you learn them on the range, chances are you're not going to hit a perfect 7-iron, only to have it end up in a trap because you didn't figure on the wind.

THIRTY MINUTES A DAY

Instead of long practice sessions, I advise my golf students to spend ten minutes three times a day practicing. Every time you can make a repetition of a swing and do it at different times, your body is going to learn that motion more quickly. Take that exercise with the parallel club I mentioned, where you hold the shaft in the middle about a foot apart and make a swing. If people would do that exercise three or four times a day—it would only take them thirty seconds to swing ten times—their big muscles would soon be trained. Not their wrists or hands, but the shoulder and back muscles. If you took someone who had never heard of golf and told him that he had to use his back and shoulders and hips and thighs to hit a golf ball, he would think you were crazy. And that's exactly why those big muscles have to be trained and developed.
— Tom Cochan, Round Hill Country Club

Every single pro I talked to, without exception, was convinced that the most important part of the game to practice was the short game. If the average golfer has taken an eight on a hole, he has probably used four of them from within 30 yards of the pin. And that's ridiculous, because it's a simple matter of practice and feel. Everybody can learn to pitch

57

and chip and putt. Basically, it's learning how far back to take the clubhead to get the ball near the pin. Here are some of the pros' suggestions for improving your short game.

Pitching. Put a bushel basket out in your backyard and stand about 15 or 20 yards away from it. Take a 9-iron and try to hit a ball over the basket. Why over it? The next time you're out on the golf course, count the number of occasions when you're past the pin on your pitch shot. You'll undoubtedly discover that you're usually short most of the time.

One way to correct this is to aim at the *middle* of the flagstick when you're 25 or 30 yards away and at the *top* of the pin when you're 50 yards or more. If you aim at the hole, you're going to end up short. That's why it's good to get the habit of hitting over the bushel basket.

GETTING A MENTAL PICTURE

When you practice, two out of every three hours should be spent in the "scoring area," that is, with clubs that you normally use when you're 75 yards or less from the green. With pitching, the most important thing in practice is to keep varying the distance of each shot. This will help you to develop a mental picture and a feel of how hard to hit each shot for a certain distance. Then when you have a similar shot out on the course, that same image should flash into your mind.

—Jim Gadino, Heritage Hill Golf Course

Within 20 yards of the green, most of my pros favored the use of the sand wedge instead of the pitching wedge. With a sand wedge there is more loft, more clubface, more room for error. If you have to pitch to an elevated green or over a bunker, a sand wedge has a definite advantage, particularly if the grass is thick and the ball sits down in it. The sand wedge will go down into the grass more easily, and even if you hit the shot a little fat, the additional weight of the club will carry the clubhead through.

Certainly, when you're in the rough, you should use a sand wedge to pitch to the green, keeping in mind the need to allow for more roll because the ball will come out without spin. If you use a pitching wedge from that spot, there's a much greater likelihood of skulling the ball. So, when you're practicing in your backyard, mark off an area with two sticks or two pieces of string, and try to make your sand wedge shots land in that cordoned-off area.

Chipping. The most important things to remember when you practice chipping are: (1) keep your feet close together; (2) keep your weight toward your left foot; (3) keep your hands slightly ahead of you; (4) when you swing, keep your left hand straight and don't bend it; (5) keep your head still. The phrase "looking up" is more a result of than a cause of a bad shot. The real culprit is lifting the upper part of the body.

When you're chipping from off the green with, say, a 5- or 6-iron, it's helpful to imagine that you have a putter in your hand. If you do, you'll probably chip with the same motion and stroke you use with long putts—taking the club-head back low to the ground. That way you'll eliminate the most common mistake made with chip shots—picking the clubhead up and stabbing down at the ball.

One of the ways to cultivate your "feel for distance" in a chip shot, namely, to learn how hard to hit the ball, is to lob a ball with your hand toward the hole—a "hand-mashie" shot, someone once called it. When you do this, you will instinctively pick a spot on the green to try to land the ball on so that it will roll up to the pin. Then substitute a

"To cultivate your 'feel for distance' . . . lob a ball with your hand toward the hole—'a hand mashie.'"

*"Make your chip shot,
trying to hit the coin."*

club for your hand and do the same thing. So, in your back-yard, it's a good idea to practice landing the ball on a precise spot, for example, into a hat. If you practice enough you'll soon develop the ability to land the ball on a preselected spot on any green.

How do you determine that spot? If you're chipping to a practice green, estimate where you want to land the ball before you hit it. Then walk to that spot and place a fifty-cent piece on it. Make your chip shot, trying to hit the coin. If you do hit close to the coin and the ball comes up 10 feet short of the pin, move the coin closer to the hole. When you hit that shot close to the coin and the ball stops 2 feet from the pin, pause for a moment and study the location of the coin. *That* spot was where you had to land the ball to get close. Get the picture securely in your mind each time, and your chipping is bound to improve.

Putting. Instinct plays a key role in putting, which is one of the reasons why there are good putters and bad putters. There are some golfers who can make nearly every green in regula-tion figures, yet who require thirty-seven or thirty-eight putts a round. There are others who never break 110, but who can two-putt most greens. Instinct plays a large part of the reason why.

For example, how far you take the clubhead back is a deliberate thing, but how you bring it forward is a matter of instinct. One of the most common faults poor putters make is taking the clubhead back too far. This inevitably leads to trouble, because when they are about to hit the ball, their instinct tells them that they have taken too big a swing and that they are going to hit the ball too hard. As a result, they ease up, or stop, or jab at the ball, instead of "releasing" the clubhead and letting it roll the ball. If they took the clubhead back a short distance, they could then let their instinct take over and hit the ball firmly.

One way of seeing to it that your backstroke is not too long is to put a tin can on the ground about 6 inches behind your putter blade as you are addressing the ball. Now put a paper cup flat on the ground about 8 feet from your ball. The object is to hit the ball into the paper cup without letting your putter touch the can. As you will find out, this not only limits your backswing, but it forces you to hit the ball with firmness, confidence, and a complete follow-through.

Putting practice can take place right in your own living room. According to the pros, the two other most important elements that determine whether you will putt well or poorly are (1) making sure you bring the putter blade absolutely straight back without altering the blade angle, and (2) keeping your body perfectly still, especially your head. When you move your body or head, you invariably change the angle of the blade and either push or pull the putt.

DON'T MOVE THAT HEAD!

In my opinion, the most important thing to remember in putting is to keep the head steady. Moving your head off line is bound to throw the blade of the putter off line, and you won't hit the putt solidly. Always keep the blade of the putter as close to the ground as possible. If you pick it up, you're going to hit down on the ball and put spin on it, usually side spin that will throw the ball off line.

With long putts distance is a more difficult thing to judge than direction. Most people don't have any trouble aiming the ball, but they don't know how hard to hit it. So, once you have established the correct line, the last thing that should be in your mind is how hard you're going to hit the ball.

—Jim Gadino, Heritage Hills Golf Course

To develop the habit of bringing the clubhead back straight each time, try this simple device. Place two clubs on your living room rug side by side and about half an inch wider apart than the width of your putter. Put a ball exactly between them. Now practice bringing the putter blade back and hitting the ball *without touching either of the parallel clubs.*

The next step is to put two other clubs, parallel to each other and about 20 feet to your left and exactly in line with the first two clubs. Put a small glass flat between them. Once again, hit the ball without touching the clubs, and this time make it roll between the far clubs so that it comes to a stop just *before* it hits the glass. Now you are practicing both distance and direction.

DON'T BE A JABBER!

Let's face it, putting is feel. You take a wrist putter, an arm putter, a hand-and-arm putter, they're all different. But I have the same advice for all of them: Make sure the putter blade is square to the ball—when you take it back and when you hit it. You'll learn through practice that when you take the blade back a foot, the ball will go only so far, depending on the green. And when you take it back 6 inches, it will go another defined distance. It's important to keep your backswing as short as possible. The longer it is, the more that can go wrong, the greater the chance of turning the blade one way or the other. Don't be a jabber, but keep your backswing short and stroke the ball firmly.

With long putts I tell my golfers to think of the pin as being surrounded by a pit that is a yard from the pin on all sides. Don't even think of getting your very long putts in the hole, just within that yard radius. The best putter I ever knew was the late Horton Smith and his advice for spending time on putting greens was: Practice 4-foot putts. His theory

"Now *practice bringing the putter blade back and hitting the ball* without touching either of the parallel clubs."

was that from 50 or 60 feet out, you should be able to get to within 4 feet of the pin. If you can make a 4-foot putt consistently, you'll make a lot of bogeys and pars, even a few birdies.

—Vince Paccadolmi, Waccabuc Country Club

Finally, there is a kind of practicing that does not require a driving range, a living-room rug, a backyard, or even a golf club. It can be done sitting behind a desk or in an easy chair, on a train, or while driving a car. All it requires is the use of your mind and your ability to create images.

There are two main phases in learning how to hit a golf ball properly. The first is forming a mental picture of a golf swing, from beginning to end, in slow motion. That's the part most high-handicap golfers overlook. The second phase is the training of specific muscles to perform the actions in that mental image. The whole process might be termed "developing muscle memory." The problem with most poor golfers is how to get to the second phase without doing the first.

And that's the reason so many golfers stand on the first tee with their minds blank, utterly at a loss as to what to do, mainly because they have never really developed an image of a golf swing in their minds, let alone trained their muscles to transform that image into reality. Naturally, their muscles don't know what to do. The muscles have not read the instruction manual.

But it's an easy thing to do, and there's no danger of overexertion. Try it while you're driving to work, or waiting for the steak to be done. Form a picture of yourself addressing a golf ball. How far away are you standing from it? How far apart are your feet? How much bend is there in your arms, your knees? Now start your backswing very slowly. What moves first? What muscles are you using? How does the clubhead look at the top of your backswing? Where is your weight?

Bring the clubhead down. What did you move first? Where is your right elbow? Where is your weight at the moment you hit the ball? Picture yourself with a full follow-through, then hold it. Look down over your left shoulder. Can you see the top of the back of your right foot? You should be able to.

Put yourself mentally about 20 yards from a green you know well. The pin is located 15 feet from the back edge, and you know that the green slopes from right to left. How far to the right of the pin do you have to aim to compensate for the slope? Where exactly do you want the ball to land? How high do you want it to go? What club would you select to enable you to achieve that arc? If you do hit it that way, how far is the ball going to roll? If you can answer such questions *before* you reach the golf course, then you will not be facing the real test with an empty mind and a wish and a prayer.

The cliché goes clattering along that "practice makes perfect." But it's not true in golf, where there is no such thing as perfection. Practice does, however, mean improvement.

The great Ben Hogan, once leading a tournament after shooting a 66, was found out in the gathering dusk hitting 9-irons to the green. When asked why he was still practicing after such a sensational round, Hogan answered, "You know, there's really no reason why I shouldn't be able to birdie *every* hole."

So, duffer, take heart. It's a strange game, this game of golf, challenging and frustrating as hell, all in one. But the memory of that one crisply hit 4-iron, or that 3-wood dead to the stick, or that long snake of a putt that just curled in, is always enough to bring you out for still another whack at it. As one pro told me, "I've been giving lessons for twenty-

67

seven years, and in all that time I've never known one person, no matter how horrendous his score, who said that he was going to give up the game of golf—and actually went ahead and did it."

If the Romans had ever played the game of golf, they would have been heard shouting: *"Capita supra ante me!"* ("Heads up, in front of me!") Today, we're more to the point. We just holler, "Fore!"

6

The Swing: Part II

*Lead back with the left shoulder, and lead down with
the left hip.*

It was a glum Harvey that showed up at the practice tee the
following Monday. He came slowly, almost dragging his
feet, as though dreading the next hour.

"Morning, Harvey. How did it go?"

"Not so good," he said with a weak smile. "I've never
been so discouraged."

"Did you get a chance to practice?"

"Every single day." He shook his head. "A fat lot of good
it did. I also did what you suggested and swung a club several
times each day. In fact, my wife now thinks I'm crazy."

I tried not to smile. "Why?"

"One night at the dinner table, all of a sudden my mind's a complete blank. I can't picture a swing, a shoulder turn, nothing. So right in the middle of dinner—my wife's going on about her brother, who I can't stand, incidentally —I get up and put a club behind my back and hold it with my elbows. Then I take a backswing—you know, like you showed me—so that the end of the club is pointing down at the ball.

"When I get back to the table, my wife says, 'What, are you exercising to get a better appetite?'

"So I tell her I was working on my shoulder turn.

"And she says, 'Your what?'

" 'My shoulder turn.'

"She gives me a real funny look and says, 'Harvey, I love you, but you're sick, sick, sick.' "

"She just joined the club," I told him. "Millions of women who don't play the game are married to golf nuts."

"And that's not the end of it. Just before I went to sleep that same night, she turns to me and says, 'Harvey, how about working on your shoulder turn now?'

" 'Ha! Ha! Ha! Very funny,' " I told her. " 'Now go to sleep.' "

I couldn't help laughing. "Don't worry about it. She'll get used to it."

"The trouble is that it didn't help much. Nothing did. I'm still not hitting the ball worth a damn."

I asked him to take a couple of practice swings and he did, swinging easily.

"That looks pretty good."

"There's something I meant to ask you. Should I pause at the top of my backswing?"

"Let me ask you a question by way of an **answer. If** you're in your car and moving forward about five miles per hour, and you shift into reverse, what happens?"

He thought for a moment. "The car slows down, stops for a second, then starts backward."

"Right. It has to stop for a fraction of a second because *it's changing direction*. Well, at the top of your backswing you're changing the direction of your swing, so you also have to pause fractionally. You may not even be conscious of it, but unless you're swinging much too fast, you'll do it automatically."

KNOWING WHAT THE RIGHT HAND IS DOING

The swing consists of three main body elements: The upper body, which puts the club in position to hit the ball; the lower body, which provides the power in hitting the ball; and the hands, which have to square the clubface off at the moment of impact.

The first part is achieved by leading the clubhead back with the left shoulder, which probably has the farthest distance to travel. You transfer weight, complete your hip turn, all while you're bringing your hands down. You hit with your right hand—I like to say that you lead with your left hand and hit with your right. Don't worry about using too much right hand. If you're swinging properly, you won't be able to use too much right hand.

—Vince Paccadolmi, Waccabuc Country Club

Harvey's practice swings looked very good. He was taking the clubhead straight back, making a pretty fair shoulder turn, and finishing nice and high. I suggested he hit a few, so he teed up a ball, picked his target, and addressed the ball.

"Hold it right there," I told him. "Don't move. Now let the club drop between your legs." He did. "Remember, I told you that the spot on the shaft where the grip starts should be near your left heel? Where is it now?"

71

He looked down. "I'll be damned. It's in front of my left toe."

"Yes. When you took your practice swings, you were relaxed and loose enough to stand comfortably at the right distance away. But once you actually faced the shot, you tensed up and fell right back into your old habit of reaching for the ball. No wonder you've been having trouble hitting it well. Move closer. Relax and let your arms hang naturally. Think of that commuter coming home from work. Are you comfortable? Now you can hit it, nice and easy."

He hit several, and they all sliced badly. "See what I mean?" he said wearily. "Same old slice."

"Hit one more and hold it at the end of your follow-through."

When he did, I asked him to look down at his feet. "Where is your weight right now, at the end of your swing?"

"On my right foot." He sounded surprised.

"Exactly. That's because you're not transferring your weight from right to left. Fire and fall back. Remember?"

"Sweet Jesus!" he said in disgust. "There are so God-damn many things to remember."

"One at a time, Harvey. Get one thing firmly in your mind before you go on to the next."

I told him to grip the club as he would a baseball bat and hit an imaginary baseball. When he did that, he automatically transferred his weight from right foot to left.

"For some reason people have no trouble with weight transfer when they're hitting a baseball. Now gradually lower the arc of your baseball swing until the clubhead is close to the ground."

I walked around behind him and held his head steady. "Keep swinging. Now you're doing it right. The main difference in transferring weight in a baseball swing and a golf swing is that in golf you have to keep your head still, or you'll

"Now gradually lower the arc of
your baseball swing until the
clubhead is close to the ground."

end up swaying. Keep swinging until you get the feel of it. As you complete the downswing, let your right knee come over and touch your left knee. That's right. Now the weight is on your left foot where it's supposed to be."

LOOK AT THAT BASEBALL SWING!

People talk about someone having a bad "baseball swing." I don't know what they mean. I have found out that if a person was a good baseball or softball player, he usually turned out to be a pretty fair golfer, because he had learned long ago the importance of transferring weight when you hit a ball, any ball, a baseball, tennis ball, soccer ball, or golf ball.

I get kids who play Little League Baseball, and when they take a golf lesson, all I do in the beginning is hold their head so that it doesn't move laterally, and tell them to swing like they would if they were hitting a baseball that was pitched at their feet. They catch on right away.

But you have to keep your head still. Take a few practice swings with the sun at your back. From just looking at your shadow on the ground, you can see whether your head is moving. If your head moves backward, you're swaying. If it moves forward, you're starting the swing from the top, not with a hip turn. Keep taking slow practice swings until you can see that the shadow of your head remains absolutely still.

—Robert Cloughan, Ridgewood Country Club

Harvey seemed to have gotten the idea of weight transfer, for now when he hit the ball, he made solid contact. There was still a bit of a slice, but the ball was getting good distance. I could almost see his confidence building. He finally hit a ball and made as good a swing as he had ever made. There was that satisfying "click" at impact, and the ball sailed straight and true. It must have traveled 230 yards.

Harvey looked up with a big grin. "Oh, boy! I really hit that one."

"You hit it flush, all right."

His next shot was a low screamer with a huge slice. Harvey looked at me, completely baffled. I could understand totally. How could he hit a perfect shot in one instant and a perfectly terrible one in the next? Welcome to the club, Harvey.

"You got overeager," I told him. "You just couldn't wait to hit another one just like that last one. You must have swung a hundred ninety miles per hour. Your swing looked just like a rattrap. Slow down. That way you'll let your club-head catch up with your body turn."

HAVE A SENSE OF TEMPO!

There is a time requirement with every golf shot. If it takes you two seconds to hit an 8-iron, it should take you four seconds to hit a driver. With a driver you have a much larger arc and a longer swing. It just takes a longer time to make a proper swing. That's one of the duffers' problems. Most of them can hit a 7-iron. So they try and hit a 3-iron or a driver in the same length of time they hit a 7-iron. And it can't be done.

They have no sense of tempo. They are what I call "directors"; they pick up the club and beat it down, "directing" the clubhead at the ball. They have to develop, instead, the feeling of passing through the ball.

A lot of people don't know how to finish a shot. They either punch at the ball and don't complete the follow-through, or they fall away from the ball and end up on their right foot. To get them to transfer weight and complete the swing, I ask them to look down over their right shoulder at the end of the shot and see if they can see the back of their right shoe. If they can, they've probably followed through properly.

—Tom Murphy, Sleepy Hollow Country Club

Harvey and I must have worked for another full hour. We took each club, one by one, from the 9-iron through the driver. He had the most trouble with the long irons—and he was in good company. I told him that most people had trouble with long irons. He also made very common errors with the other clubs. At one point he asked me to enumerate the most common errors with each club. I told him that that had been one of the questions I had put to my pros. Here is their consensus, and the ways to overcome these faults:

Driver. The most common fault with a driver is trying to hit it too hard. As a result, the timing is off. One of the best ways to correct this is to swing the driver more slowly and easily than any other club—or to use a 3-wood instead. The high-handicap golfer has one great misconception: that distance is the important thing. Yet a good player could probably shoot a round in the 80s with nothing in his bag higher than a 5-iron.

Fairway Woods. One main trouble with hitting woods in the fairway is failure to get "down" to the ball. The high-handicap golfer often still conceives of the shot as being a ball on a tee, because he's using a wood. As a result, he tops the ball. Suggestion: Use a more lofted club. Why try to hit a 2-wood off the fairway when it's so much easier to hit a 5-wood? Another common fault is trying to steer the ball to the green, instead of relaxing the hands and body and just swinging the club.

Long Irons. The most common fault with these clubs is false expectations. The average golfer knows that a 2- or 3-iron

76

is supposed to go 180 or 190 yards. It's a "distance iron," isn't it? So he is determined to make it go a great distance, and he takes a mighty swipe at it. What happens shouldn't happen to any golfer.

There's another common misconception. For some reason, many high-handicap golfers think that you have to swing hard to get loft, that the harder they hit the ball, the higher it will go. But, Jack Nicklaus notwithstanding, 2- and 3-irons are not supposed to go very high, and a nice easy swing will give the ball the arc it should have.

For most golfers, long irons are the hardest clubs to hit, so the very act of hitting them becomes largely a mental problem. But if you can convince yourself that you're really holding a 5- or 6-iron and only want to hit the ball that far, you'll swing easier and with more confidence—and you may be surprised at the results.

Middle Irons. The most common fault with middle irons— 4, 5, and 6—is underclubbing. Most high-handicap golfers tend to remember the good shots they've made, perhaps because they are few and far between, and forget the bad ones. If a person has once hit a 6-iron, say, 165 yards, he will immediately pull out that club when he's 165 yards from the green. But the chances are that he will *not* hit that 6-iron perfectly. It makes more sense to hit a 4- or 5-iron and make the green even if the shot is only hit moderately well.

Short Irons. With poor golfers, the most common fault with these clubs is trying to lift the ball, to get under it, to scoop it off the ground. And because they're trying to get under the ball, they lean to the rear and their weight stays on their right foot. When this happens, the clubhead hits the ground to the right of the ball, and they end up taking a big divot *before* they reach the ball. What they have to realize is that

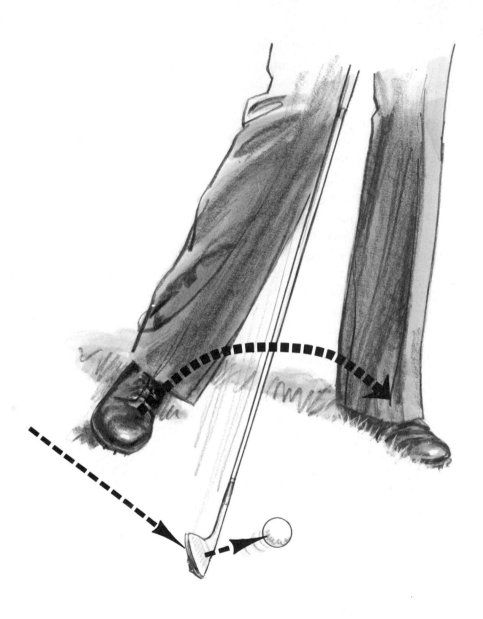

"Only if you hit down and let your weight transfer, will the ball go up in the air."

only by hitting down and letting their weight transfer will the ball go up in the air.

FORGET THE PIN!

One of the most common faults in hitting short irons to the green is that the average golfer sees only the pin. It may be lying next to a trap, or on a steep decline, but he hits right at it. The fact is that only very good golfers should do that because it requires exceptional control. The average golfer should forget about pin placement when he's 75 yards or more from the green. Instead, he should hit for the center, or fat part of the green, so he won't end up in the bunker when he makes a slight mistake.

—Jim Gadino, Heritage Hills Golf Club

Toward the end of our practice session, Harvey confessed that he had always had great difficulty getting out of traps.

"I get psyched by traps," he said. "I just don't know how to hit a bunker shot. If I land in the trap, I'm bound to lose two or three strokes before I'm done with it."

"Actually, any good golfer will tell you that a trap shot is really quite an easy shot to make," I told him.

"Not for me." Harvey shook his head. "They're murder."

"The putting green has a small trap on one side of it. Why don't we walk over, and I'll see if I can show you the basics."

As we were walking over to the putting green, I told Harvey the most common mistake made by duffers when they found themselves in a trap.

"When they swing, they usually stop; they don't follow through," I said. "They just haven't got the mental picture

"Take a full swing and hit that little pie with marshmallow intact and complete your swing."

of how the shot should look, like you. Yet all they have to remember is to hit two inches behind the ball and try and knock it over the green. That will help them to follow through."

When we got to the trap, I asked Harvey to take a few practice swings and imagine that he was hitting a ball. "Open your clubface and your stance so that your left foot is back a little. Take your normal short-iron swing."

He swung a few times. In each case, he dug down into the sand and the clubhead stopped.

"It is essential that you follow through, Harvey," I told him. "You'll never get out of a trap until you learn to finish your swing."

Soon he began doing that, finishing nicely. I threw a ball into the trap and told him to hit it with the same motion he had just been using. He took a big swing and hit down at the ball. The sand wedge buried itself in the sand. The ball did not move.

"That's what always happens," he muttered.

"Follow through, Harvey."

He swung again. This time he didn't hit any sand and he completed his swing. Unfortunately, he picked the ball cleanly off the sand and it flew way over the green.

"That's one way to get out," he said ruefully.

"You'll keep doing that as long as you keep thinking of the clubhead hitting the ball. You have to realize that with a bunker shot it's the force of the sand coming up off the clubface that lifts the ball. The club itself should never make contact with the ball. One pro told me that he asks his students to think of a small pot pie with a marshmallow sitting on top of it. What he tells them to do is to take a full swing and hit that little pie with marshmallow intact and complete their swing."

"I'll try to think of it that way," he said. And apparently

81

he succeeded. Of the twenty balls he hit, all but four of them at least made it out of the trap.

"My God!" he said when he had finished. "I honestly think I can get out of a trap now."

"You probably can," I assured him. "For one thing, you don't have a mental block about it any more. The main reason people can't get out of traps is because they don't *think* they can get out. They've never developed the image of a good trap shot, and they panic. If they could simply learn to follow through, most of their troubles in sand would vanish."

"How about going out on the course next week and really playing?" he asked, almost like a kid asking for dessert.

"You think you're ready for the real thing?"

"I'll practice all week, then next Monday . . ." He shrugged. "We'll find out how much I've learned anyhow."

And how much you still have to learn, I thought, but I didn't say it. Harvey, at that point, was like the man who has just learned how to tread water. After doing it for 10 minutes, he said, "It sure keeps you afloat, but the trouble is you don't go anywhere."

7

Drive for Show
and Putt for Dough

If you try to fight the course, it will beat you.
—Lou Graham

Harvey and I played golf the following Monday—and for the next ten weeks. We played at least once a week, sometimes twice, always preceded by a twenty- to thirty-minute warm-up on the practice tee and putting green. Harvey also continued to practice, both on the range, by himself on the course, and in his own backyard. I don't know to this day how all this golf affected his marriage, particularly his "shoulder turns" at night, but there was no doubt that there was a dramatic improvement in his golf score.

Over that period of time, we accomplished two things: Harvey began to develop muscle memory. Despite the numerous lapses in concentration, regressions, and just plain dumb shots, he gradually acquired a certain acceptable groove to his swing and a resulting confidence in his ability to hit more good shots than bad. The second accomplishment resulted from his learning a crucial fact: to turn in a decent score, he had to *think* on the golf course and use whatever devices are necessary to force thinking. Harvey's change for the better convinced me beyond any doubt that, given proper instruction and the will to play good golf, *anyone* can do what Harvey did.

The week before, Harvey had bought a new set of woods, and his club selection was indicative of his new frame of mind. For he had discarded his driver and 2-wood and had settled on Investment Casting irons and 3-, 4-, 5-, and 6-woods. He had received the message and had decoded it: What purpose is distance if you can only hit the driver one out of five times and keep it in the fairway?

THE RIGHT CLUBS FOR YOU

I'm a great believer in Investment Casting—the new Pings and Links clubs, for example. I think they have done more for the inept player than anything else. For one thing, they get the ball up in the air if you make contact. That's because the center of gravity in the clubs is now lower.

Also, they utilize a new concept for golf equipment. There are many people who believe that the average golf club is poorly designed in terms of weight distribution. Why do you need all that weight in the back of the club? It's fine if you can hit the ball in the center of the clubhead every time, but your duffer can't do that. Investment Casting clubs have been built on the balanced-weight concept where the weight is distributed evenly between heel and toe. So, when the average golfer hits the ball on the toe or heel of the clubhead, the club doesn't turn in his hand. There's weight where he hit it. There's no question that the poorer player has to play better with such clubs.

I know through experience that most people are playing with clubs that are much too heavy for them. Too many stores only carry heavy clubs. And there's no doubt that heavy clubs are much harder to swing and control. Also, you

don't need heavy clubs to get distance. Baseball players have proved that they can generate more bat speed with lighter bats. All your good golfers, including the touring pros, are now swinging lighter clubs. And Pings and Links are light. That's why I think they're good for duffers.
—Tom Murphy, Sleepy Hollow Country Club

Our first two outings on the course were more an extension of our sessions on the practice tee than recordable rounds of serious golf. We didn't even bother to keep score. That wasn't the purpose. During those initial two sessions, what I tried to do was fix in Harvey's mind what I had learned from my pros—and had previously passed along to him. I endeavored by constant repetition to keep the graphic tips *graphic*, and the things to remember easily *memorable*.

During those two rounds, I also discovered Harvey's great weakness, and one which had escaped me on the practice tee —his burning impatience. Once he got the idea in his mind of how to make a swing and hit a shot, he simply could not fathom the inability of his body to perform what his mind told it to do. But old habits die hard. He fell into his bad old habits quite easily, especially when he became angry at himself or impatient with his progress. "X-rated" words frequently seared the sedate fairways, and whirling unaccompanied clubs made their own peculiar divots. Still, Harvey began to gain some control over his temper, and soon I began not to flinch involuntarily when we approached a foursome of women who had graciously allowed us to play through.

By the third outing, I decided that he should have a visible record of his accomplishment, whether it be for smug perusal or for burning. His previous low had been 112, but he admitted that his average round had been in "the neighborhood" of 120. Obviously, a deteriorating neighborhood. How many strokes could he shave from that? He wanted very much to know. So did I. We would go for score—I hoped.

So it was that when we stepped up onto that first tee on that third Monday in May, Harvey held a 3-wood in his hands—and perhaps visions of sugarplum fairies in his head. He was loose, I assumed, since he had already hit about twenty-five balls off the practice tee. Once more the cigar was clamped between his teeth, and by the way he gripped the club as he addressed the ball, I could see how determined he was.

Too determined. "Harvey, you're going to strangle that club," I said gently. "Pretend you're shaking hands with a great lady—very tenderly."

He smiled, stepped away from the ball, took a deep breath and a slow practice swing. Then he stepped up, waggled the clubhead a few times, and hit the ball. It wasn't a bad shot, but he must have been a little nervous, for the ball sliced and ended up in the right rough about 200 yards out. I hit a good drive down the middle. (From now on, since my own golf game is significant only when it touches on the way Harvey plays, we'll keep the number one TV camera focused exclusively on our paunchy middle-aged anti-hero.)

Harvey considered his next shot, standing behind the ball, his eye on the green. He was about 155 yards away, in the rough, with a so-so lie.

"I want to hit a seven- or eight-iron, but I know that's just my instinct," he said. "You see how I've learned? I think I'll hit a five and not swing too hard."

"Good decision, Harvey," I told him. "It's also important when you're in the rough to make sure you hit the ball first, not the grass. So play the ball a little more off your right foot."

He didn't hit the ball very well, but it was good enough

so that he ended up about 15 yards in front of the green. When we reached that spot, I said, "It's a good idea, whenever you get within twenty or twenty-five yards of the green, to count the number of strokes it takes you to get in the hole from that distance. You might even keep a separate scorecard on it."

"Why? What's the point of it?"

"For one thing, it's a damn good way to find out what part of your game needs work—putting, chipping, or both. Look at it this way, Harvey. You can often make up for a topped drive, or a four-iron that was butchered. It often will take a great recovery shot, but it can be done. The important thing to remember is that once you're within twenty yards of the green, *every* shot becomes crucial. For the inescapable fact is that if you miss a two-and-a-half-foot putt, you're simply going to shoot one more for the day than if you had made that putt."

"Drive for show, putt for dough?"

"Never forget it, buddy. It's the name of the game."

He hit his chip shot, but it was not hard enough and he was 25 feet short of the pin.

"Did you pick out a spot to land on?" I asked him.

He grinned sheepishly. "I forgot."

"Harvey, you only have one chance on each shot. Every single time you forget to think about how to hit it, and where to hit it, it's going to cost you strokes. There's no such thing as 'forgiveness' in golf. And if you ever want to break ninety, you just can't forget to think, think, THINK."

He hit a good, firm putt to within 18 inches of the hole and tapped in.

"Do you remember what you had the last time you played this hole for score?" I reminded him.

He shook his head. "I haven't the foggiest."

"I do. You took a ten. Today it took you exactly half as

many blows. You know why? Mainly, because the last time you were trying to murder the ball and today you were swinging the club. And that's what it's all about, Harvey."

The next hole was the par-five dogleg to the left. Harvey once more took his 3-wood—and regressed. He stood too far from the ball, swung fast and very hard. And he topped the ball. It dribbled out about 50 yards.

"You trying to reach the green in one?" I asked.

"Huh? Oh, you mean I swung too hard?"

"Like you were mad at the golf ball and trying to beat it to death."

"C'mon, Frank. This is a par-five. I've gotta really get it out there," he protested. "I've gotta put some muscle behind it."

"Do you really? Think about this hole for one moment. How is it constructed? You know, it's like most par-fives anywhere. And contrary to popular opinion, par-fives are *not* the hardest holes on a golf course. They are usually rated high on a handicap basis because for the average golfer there's more opportunity to make mistakes.

"The fact is that the run-of-the-mill par-five requires two easy woods, or even two long irons, plus one short-iron shot to reach the green. There's no reason for you to swing hard enough to dislocate your back. Unlike the pros, who flit across your TV screen, there is no conceivable way you are going to make the green in two shots. But—and consider this closely—if you can hit two woods no more than one hundred eighty yards each, what you will have left is *the easiest par-three on the golf course.*"

He looked surprised. "I never thought of it that way."

"Most people don't. All they can see is that green which looks miles away. And they think they really have to cream the ball to do well on the hole."

We reached his ball, and he stood considering the possibilities. He still had about 130 yards left to get to that point in the fairway where it doglegged left sharply. And an 8-iron would put him in perfect position for his next shot. He pulled out a 4-wood.

"I'm going to go over the trees," he said. "From here I think I can make it."

I didn't make any comment. This was one lesson he would have to learn on his own.

He hit the ball well, but he didn't catch all of it. The tops of the trees were in the way and the ball dropped into the woods.

"So I was wrong, Goddamn it," he said, and there was defiance in his voice. "I just wanted to see if I could do it."

"Harvey, you know you could probably do it—if you had enough tries at it. But you only had one try. That's what made it a bad-risk shot."

"What the hell is a bad-risk shot?"

"By 'bad risk' I mean two things. First, if you don't hit the shot perfectly, you'll be in trouble. Second, the kind of trouble you end up in will probably cost you more than one stroke. You had to hit your four-wood perfectly to clear those trees, and now that you're in the woods, it will probably cost you plenty. *That's* a bad-risk shot."

Harvey finally took a nine on the hole. I know. I counted every shot. But when I asked him what he got, he muttered, "Give me a seven."

"You sure?" I said softly.

"What the hell difference does it make, Frank? We're not playing a match or for money."

"It does make a difference, Harvey, and I'll tell you why. You have to be realistic about your golf. When you say you had a seven on a hole and you really had a nine, you are kid-

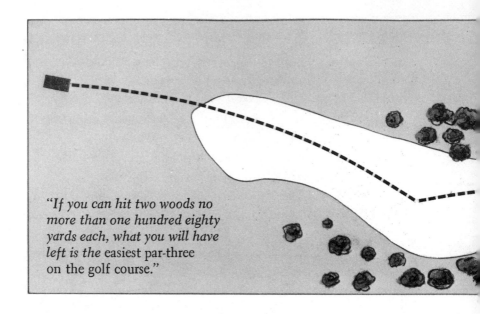

"*If you can hit two woods no more than one hundred eighty yards each, what you will have left is the easiest par-three on the golf course.*"

ding no one but yourself. And when that day comes—and it will, believe me—when you proudly mark down an 'eighty-nine,' on your scorecard, only you will know whether you conveniently forgot five or six strokes out there. And if you did, you really had a ninety-four or ninety-five, and there's no real satisfaction in bragging about your eighty-nine. Because your eighty-nine is a lie.

"There's another reason why it pays off to count all your swings at the ball. A bad shot is the result of bad thinking, and on a golf course you are penalized for stupid shots. But it's only when you accept that fact, pay the penalty for it, and resolve not to make that particular error again, that you're going to improve. As the old joke goes, 'Pay the two-dollar fine.' But remember why you're paying it."

"It just kills me to get those nines, tens, and elevens," Harvey said, sighing deeply.

"Sure it's discouraging to write down those high num-

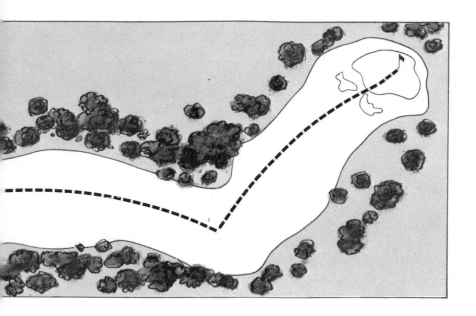

bers on the scorecard," I agreed. "But they are only reminders of the bad shots you hit. And on the next hole, when you don't repeat those errors, the four or five you put down on your card is visual reassurance that you don't have to hit dumb shots. All you have to do is concentrate. You know how the shot should be hit. Concentrate, concentrate, and you *will* hit it the right way most of the time."

"OK. The sermon worked," he said, grinning. "Give me a nine for the hole."

THE PROS KNOW

Many hackers are using equipment that is not right for them. They go to a sports store, and a salesman, who probably knows less about golf than they do, sells them equipment that is available. Usually, such clubs are too heavy and too stiff-shafted for the average player. Sometimes, there aren't two clubs in the whole set that will balance out. The result is poor players playing with poor equipment. Good golfers might be able to play with that equipment, but the poorer player doesn't have a chance.

My advice is to go to a professional when you're looking for clubs. It won't necessarily cost you any more—all pro shops have sales now and then—and your pro will be able to advise you on the swing weight, shaft flexibility, loft, grip thickness that is right for you. Personally, I don't think anyone with a handicap of 16 or more should be swinging a club heavier than a D-1.

—Jim Gadino, Heritage Hills Golf Club

Harvey played the next three holes quite well, getting two bogeys and a par. The sixth hole was a par-three, 145 yards, with a huge trap in front of it. I hit an 8-iron to the center of the green. Harvey selected a club, hesitated, then turned to me.

"What did you hit, Frank?"

"An eight-iron."

He immediately put the club he had chosen back in the bag and pulled out another one. He hit it slightly off the toe—and right into the bunker in front of the green.

As we were walking up to it, I asked him, "What club were you going to hit originally?"

"A seven-iron."

"And you changed to an eight?"

He nodded. "I figured if that's what you were using . . ."

"What does it matter what club I was hitting? I'm not you. I'm not built like you, and I don't swing quite like you. And I've been playing golf since I was eleven years old. You can't let your ego get involved in this thing, Harvey. You have to play golf within your own game. A seven-iron was probably the right club for you; a five-iron might have been right for someone else. When you hit an eight, you had to strain,

"Your putter may be your best
friend when it comes to
getting out of a trap."

and therefore you didn't hit it well. But if you thought that a seven-iron was the right club for that distance—and you did think so because you chose it at first—then it was simply false pride to hit an eight-iron, because you didn't want to be outdone. That's not smart golf, and, again, it's going to cost you."

When we reached the trap, I saw that Harvey's ball was in a nasty spot, about 8 inches from the back edge. He resolutely took out his sand wedge and tried to find a position in which he was both comfortable and balanced. It wasn't easy. His right foot was on solid ground, while his left foot was in the trap. It made him look tilted. When he swung at the ball, he was not able to get down to it and hit it with the bottom edge of the club. The ball whizzed across the trap and lodged under the far lip—an even worse spot.

It took Harvey three more blows to extricate his ball from its niche and nudge it up onto the green. But he was still 45 feet from the pin, and it took him three putts to get down.

"A lousy eight!" he growled. "Of all the lousy luck!"

"Maybe. But it was lousy luck that was predictable."

"What the hell do you mean by that?"

"Harvey, you had a very difficult trap shot, one that would have given pause to a really good player. The stance was impossible, you had very little room to work with behind the ball, and there was a huge, deep trap with a high lip to get out of. A very tough shot, especially for a guy who has just learned how to play bunker shots."

"What should I have done, prayed for help?"

"How about the idea of considering an alternative? There was no lip at the back of the trap, and you were only a couple of feet from a nice grassy area. You could have taken your putter and putted the ball out of the trap to the rear."

"You mean putt backwards?"

"Sure. Then you would have had an easy pitch shot from a grass lie. If you got it close to the pin and sank your putt, you've got your four. Even if it took you two putts, you still end up with a five. And five is three big strokes less than an eight."

"But a putter out of a trap." He shook his head in disgust.

"Harvey, I thought you wanted to break ninety. If that's your aim, you'll learn to use *any* club in any situation if it will help you save strokes."

Harvey finished the front nine with a five, six, and seven. His total for nine holes was 53, and that included an eight and a nine.

"If you could have simply bogeyed those two holes, you would have cut your score down to forty-six—and that's not bad."

"That's a big word—IF."

"Is it bigger than you, Harvey?"

He grinned. "We'll soon find out. Let's go to the tenth."

"After you, my favorite guinea pig."

SPECIAL NOTE: Investment casting irons are the latest "in" golf clubs and are truly designed to help your game by widening the "sweet spot" on the blade. Made of an extremely hard steel (#17–4), they are constructed by means of a cast, or mold. Investment casting is, literally, casting by the *cire perdue*, or lost wax, process—a process that consists of making a wax model, coating it with clay to form a mold, and heating it until the wax runs out through small holes in the mold. Molten metal is then poured into the space left vacant.

At this approximate point in the regular, or forged iron, process, the real work begins on the club—shaping, filing, buffering, and polishing. But with investment casting irons little more is done once the club comes out of the mold. That's one reason the clubs look crude and unpolished. The price, however, is not crude: about $40 more per set than forged irons.

One reason for this added expense is the "heel and toe" design, which more evenly distributes weight to the heel and toe of the blade. This makes the "sweet spot" much wider and is a boon to high-handicap golfers, giving them a much greater margin for error.

8

There Are No "Gimmes" in Golf

*Let's face it, 95 percent of this game is mental. A guy
plays lousy golf, he doesn't need a pro, he needs a
shrink.*

—Tom Murphy, Professional

The first time Harvey and I had played the tenth hole, it had
almost been the last time for him. On that 190-yard par-three
he had hit three balls in the water—and his clubs had almost
followed them. If he could have thrown them a little further,
they also would have found a watery grave.

But on this Monday, he calmly hit a 4-wood to within 10
feet of the green.

"Great shot!" I told him. "You made a fine swing."

He was beaming. "You know, I just swung easy and forgot all about the water," he said and sounded a little surprised.

"Murder is gone from your mind," I said softly.

He glanced at me. "I guess you have to pay a penalty when you play with a writer."

Up on the green, he missed his birdie putt, but he was still delighted with his three. "My first three ever on that hole," he said with satisfaction.

"It won't be your last, either."

The eleventh hole is the number-one handicap hole, a 440-yard par-four. Harvey had hit a fairly good drive with a slight fade. He was lying on the right side of the fairway about 200 yards out. When he pulled out his 3-wood, I put my hand on his arm.

"Why are you hitting a three-wood? Look up ahead."

He stared. "What am I supposed to see?"

"You're supposed to see that the fairway gets very narrow and there are woods on both sides. If you don't hit the ball perfectly straight, you'll be in trouble. And you're not going to get home, not even with a howitzer."

"But I want to get it close, so I'll have a chance to make par."

"Whose par?"

"I don't follow you."

"You raised an important point. This is a very difficult hole, the hardest on the course. For a three-, four-, or five-handicap golfer it's a legitimate and challenging par-four. But for the average golfer it has to be a par-five. And you should consider it a par-five and play it accordingly."

"How should I play it?"

"Well, up ahead about a hundred fifty yards, the fairway widens and there's a nice flat section. An easy five-iron will put you right in the middle of it. From that spot, it's only an eight- or nine-iron to the green. Two putts will give you a par. *Your* par."

97

What I was trying to get across to Harvey was the necessity of setting attainable goals. The eleventh hole was the most difficult hole on the golf course, and he should forget about making a four on it. If he scored no worse than a five, there would be many easier holes on which he could make his par-four. But Harvey's par on that hole should be five—and he had a damn good chance of making it.

That's exactly what he did, although he followed my suggestion reluctantly. But after he finished the hole, he turned to me ·and said, "You know, that hole always gave me fits. I was fighting it all the time. But when you play it that way, it's really a pretty easy hole. Maybe a five is par for me."

"It is your par," I assured him. "And you made. your par because you played the hole the smart way instead of the muscle way. Does it make you feel any less manly?"

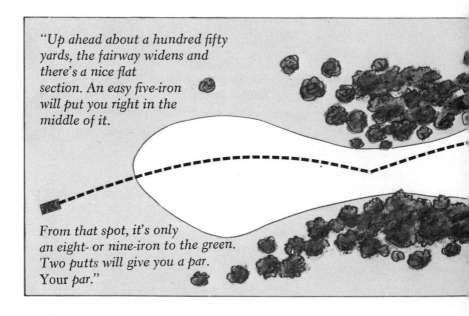

"Up ahead about a hundred fifty yards, the fairway widens and there's a nice flat section. An easy five-iron will put you right in the middle of it.

From that spot, it's only an eight- or nine-iron to the green. Two putts will give you a par. Your par."

"Hell no!" He grinned. "And it looks just fine on the scorecard."

On the next hole, a relatively easy par-four, Harvey reverted again, swinging too hard, too fast, and falling away from the ball. He hit way behind it, and the ball dribbled off the tee.

"Goddamn it!" he growled. "I play one hole real good, then do something real dumb. This Goddamn game!"

"Your mind was still back on the last two holes, savoring that three and five. It should have been on this tee, focusing on this swing, this shot. Someone once remarked that the most important shot in golf is the next shot. It's a good thing to remember, Harvey."

Out on the fairway, he concentrated this time and hit a nice 5-wood. When we reached the ball for his third shot, Harvey stood looking from his ball to the green, back and

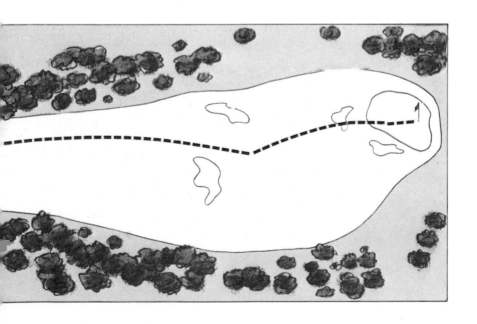

forth. He picked some bits of grass and tossed them in the air. But there was no discernible wind. He started to take an iron out of his bag, shoved it back, and looked at me.

"I have absolutely no idea what to hit. I've never been in this spot before."

I looked toward the green, and since I've been playing golf a long time, I'm a pretty fair judge of distance.

"I would say that you're a hundred eighty yards away," I told him.

He nodded. "That's about a five-wood for me. I almost hit a five-iron." He hit the 5-wood, and although he sliced it a bit, it was hole high. In other words, it was the right club for him from that distance.

As we were walking up to the green, I told Harvey about a technique used by one of the pros I talked with. Whenever he gives a playing lesson, he advises his student to stop at various points around the golf course, look at the green, and ask himself, "If my ball were here, what club would I use?" Then the pro tells him the approximate distance so that the student can verify his imaginary club selection.

"This pro feels that if you keep doing that, at one point your ball *will* be lying at the same distance, and you'll know what club to hit," I explained. "You'll eventually learn what club is right for you at any distance. Pay no attention to what other people are hitting at specific distances. It may influence you adversely. Only you know how far you can hit a three-iron, a seven-iron, or a four-wood. And once you've learned to judge distance, you've got it made."

The next hole was a deceiving par-four. Although it was only 330 yards long, a large brook ran across the fairway. It started on the left about 170 yards out and crossed the fairway at an angle so that it was 210 yards away on the right.

As Harvey pulled out his 3-wood, I murmured, "A bad-risk shot, Harvey."

"I always hit a wood here. I know I can get across if I play it to the left," he pointed out.

"When you hit your woods, what are you likely to do?"

"Well, I still have a little slice," he admitted.

"Exactly. And if you do slice, your ball will come down to the right where the brook is over two hundred yards away. On the other hand, what will you gain if you do manage to clear the brook? You'll be hitting an eight- or nine-iron, instead of a five or six. But it's still a gamble, and for what you'll gain, it's a bad gamble in my opinion."

Harvey finally saw the logic and hit a good solid 4-iron. It sliced a little and landed on the right side of the fairway, about 20 yards short of the brook. He hit a 6-iron to just in front of the green. On his chip shot, he made the mistake of lifting the upper part of his body, and skulled the ball to the back of the green. Still, with two putts, he had his five.

I told him, "If you had gone in the brook, there's little likelihood you would have made a five, and you might even have taken an eight or nine. But you got a five even with a mishit shot. Didn't it make sense to play safe?"

"It made sense," he admitted. "But it's an awful temptation to go for broke off the tee."

"If you want to break ninety consistently," I said slowly, "it's a temptation you're going to have to resist—consistently."

In the middle of the fairway on the following hole, Harvey stood too far from the ball and made a hands-and-arms swing at it—his old form. The ball went off the toe of the club and shot into the underbrush on the right. Muttering to himself, Harvey strode toward it. Before going after him, I took a stick and rammed it into the ground where his ball had been.

When we finally located his ball, it was nestling in the heart of tangled underbrush. Sighing, Harvey took out an 8-

iron and leaned down to part the branches, prepared to do battle.

"Do you think you can get out of there in one shot?" I asked him.

"Christ! I may never get out," he growled. "This is thick stuff."

"Then why try?"

He straightened and stared at me. "You mean I should quit?"

"Of course not. But why not declare an unplayable lie?"

"But that will cost me strokes."

"And you think trying to hack your way out of there won't cost you strokes? Harvey, you could swing three or four times in that stuff, and even if you did get out, you would probably still be in the rough. But if you declare an unplayable lie, you could drop your ball in the fairway and all it would cost you would be a one-stroke penalty."

"One stroke? In the fairway?"

"You see that stick out there? That's where you hit your ball from. Now draw an imaginary line between that stick and your present lie. You can drop your ball at any point along that line."

"*Any* point?"

"Any point. Even from the same spot you hit it from originally."

"You mean I'll just be hitting three?"

"No. Your second shot went in here. A one-stroke penalty means that you're now lying three, but out in the fairway. You'll be hitting your fourth shot."

Without hesitation, Harvey picked up his ball and carried it out to the fairway where he dropped it. "That's just like the bankruptcy law," he said, grinning. "It gives you a fresh start in life."

Harvey had just discovered an important aspect of the

game that all too many golfers ignore—being realistic about their ability to perform "miracle shots." When they are a couple of inches from a tree, or next to a fence, or deep in the woods, they suddenly imagine they are all Lee Trevinos and can pull off a professional shot. And sure, there's always a chance they can get lucky and knock the ball out onto the fairway. But, again, it's a low-percentage shot, a bad-risk shot. And there's a much better alternative—to declare an unplayable lie.

Many golfers do not take advantage of this rule because (a) they hate to give up an automatic stroke, or (b) they aren't quite sure how the rule works, or (c) they still believe in miracles. Yet, they should consider the options. Should they elect to hit their ball from deep in the woods, they may end up refighting the Battle of Belleau Woods. But for one stroke, they are *sure* to be hitting their next shot from the fairway (assuming they started from the fairway).

At one point Harvey and I were held up by several groups of golfers in front of us and had to wait on the tee. Just as we were about to tee off, the threesome behind us approached the tee and stood quietly watching. I hit a good drive, but as Harvey stood up to address his ball, I could see he was visibly nervous in front of this unexpected audience. As he was addressing the ball, he accidentally knocked it off the tee.

Muttering to himself, he teed up again—and promptly forgot everything he had learned. His backswing was a blur, he fell away from the ball, and topped it about 60 yards down the fairway. His face red, Harvey walked quickly to the ball, took another mighty swing—and topped it. His third shot at least got up into the air but sliced badly into the right rough.

When we were about 250 yards out, I stopped him and said, "Let's see what that threesome behind us does."

We watched as they hit. The first guy hit a tremendous

slice into the woods, and his provisional ball followed it. The second guy hit one of those famous "300-yard" drives—100 yards up, 100 yards out, and 100 yards down. The third member dribbled it off the tee and ended up in the left rough.

"You see where they all went?" I asked him, and he nodded. "What does that tell you?"

"I don't know what you're getting at."

"Their tee shots should tell you that those three golfers are no better than you are; in fact, they're probably much worse. There's no sense in trying to impress them, or being nervous in front of them, or trying to rush your shot, or even *thinking* of them. Take your time and shut them out of your mind. Concentrate on what *you* are doing, not on what they are not doing."

"You give me more orders than my wife," he said with a chuckle.

"They're not orders, Harvey. They're just suggestions."

"Sure, sure," he said sarcastically. "That's what she calls them too."

When he finished, Harvey had carded three, five, seven, four, five, six, eight, seven, five for a 50 on the back nine. He had ended up with 103, seventeen shots better than his previous "average" and a full nine strokes better than he had ever done before. He was delighted.

As we were having a beer on the nineteenth hole, I told him to study his scorecard. "You can learn a hell of a lot from it. And you're still a long way from breaking ninety."

We checked the separate score he had kept on the number of shots it had taken him to get down from within 20 yards of the pin. It had required fifty-two strokes.

"A good golfer expects to get down in two when he's that close to the pin. That means you were sixteen over the ideal number. It also means you still need a lot of work on your short game, chipping, and putting. Better get to the putting green and start using your backyard and living-room rug."

"Yes, sir. Aye, aye, admiral."

I also showed Harvey how each hole could tell him something, as it can tell you. For example, look at the par-threes. How many threes and fours did you score on these short holes? If you scored five or more, what was the main reason? Were you using the wrong club to reach the green? Try to visualize the hole in your mind. Was there a smart or safe way to play it—and you chose the dumb way? What club will you use and how will you play it next time?

I've already mentioned that the par-fives are not the hardest holes, if you don't try to murder the ball. If you took eights and nines on those par-fives, you still haven't realized the correct way to play long holes. Take it easy and just play each shot one at a time.

And with the long par-fours, if you're scoring sevens and eights, you haven't yet been realistic about what is par for you. Consider those holes par-fives to be realistic, and you won't strain a gut trying to get home in two shots.

With short par-fours, there is usually some sort of trouble on the hole—bunkers, water, sloping fairways, doglegs, tiny greens—to compensate for the shorter yardage. Look at your scorecard. If those were the holes that gave you trouble, it may be because you conveniently forgot that "trouble," or were psyched by it, or thought too highly of your ability to conquer it. Those are the holes where you should score well, and if you didn't, try playing them a little differently next time. If you tried to carry a stream or a pond and didn't make it, play safe next time. If it took you three blows to get out of the big trap to the right of the seventh green, next time

105

play your approach shot to the left side of the green. The sixteenth fairway slopes to the left, so next time aim your drive right and "play the roll."

Never mind your ego or your macho! There's no room on the scorecard for you to write: "Four—and I cleared the water." There are no descriptive phrases for the cold numbers on your card. You can't put down: "Seven—but I hit a 250-yard drive," or, "Eight—but I dropped a long putt." Start using your head instead of your heft and watch your score drop.

Compare the scores for your separate nines. Are they very different? If you had a 58 on the front nine and came in with a 49, chances are you were not properly warmed-up, either mentally or physically. Next time, hit a few golf balls and spend some time on the putting green, putting and chipping. If you shot a 48 going out and a 57 on the back nine, it could have been caused by several things. For one thing, you might be out of shape and have begun to tire around the thirteenth or fourteenth hole. If that's the case, a little daily exercise would help.

Or, you might have developed a bad habit on the course. Maybe, in the beginning, you were swinging slow and easy, and as the day went on, you got faster and faster, thus destroying all your timing and rhythm. Or, perhaps you tried to correct a fault and began overcompensating for it. It might be a good idea to take a break between nines the next time. Your scorecard can tell you a great many things—other than how much money you won or lost.

Exactly five weeks later, Harvey stood on the eighteenth green, facing a 3-foot putt.

"That's good, isn't it?" he asked hopefully. "That's a gimme, isn't it?"

"There are no gimmes in golf. The game is played from tee to cup. Knock it in, Harvey."

He stood over it, lining up carefully, and stroked it firmly into the back of the cup—for an 89.

"Hot damn!" he said jubilantly. "I did it! I broke ninety."

"Congratulations. And you did it legitimately—with no mulligans, gimmes, or 'forgotten' shots. You counted every time you swung at the ball and you still broke ninety. Now we have to get you to do it consistently."

But that was easier said than done.

Harvey couldn't wait until the next week to play again. He figured he had it licked and wanted to prove it. So we played Thursday, and Harvey had a 97. He was in a state of shock when he finished, and he had good reason to be. On that particular day, he had forgotten much of what he had learned. He could do nothing right. I knew that it was time for another session on the practice tee and a review of basics.

It was either that—or taking him to a shrink.

9

Back to the Old Drawing Board

After an abominable round of golf, a man is known to have slit his wrists with a razor blade and, having bandaged them, to have stumbled into the locker room and inquired of his partner, "What time tomorrow?"
—Alistair Cooke

The very next day found Harvey and me back on the practice tee. Harvey had blamed his poor round on confusion, on his inability to remember so many things to do and not to do.

"In golf, it's impossible to keep more than one thing in your mind at a time," I had reminded him. "The secret is to keep thinking of just one thing every time you swing. Concentrate on that one positive act and keep doing it until it's solidly in your mind and your body, or until you've achieved *muscle memory* with that one aspect. Then go on to the next thing to learn and remember."

We spent an hour and a half on the tee that day, going over basics, restressing all the things I had worked on with him. I'll give them to you just as I went over them with Harvey.

Grip. A good grip is essential to playing good golf. If your grip is wrong, nothing you can do will compensate for it for very long. For your grip largely determines at what angle the clubhead meets the ball, hence what direction it will go.

It is important that the hands are placed on the club so that they are exactly lined up with the clubhead as it rests on the ground. One way to achieve this is to grip the shaft right next to the clubhead. When your hands and the clubhead are only an inch or two apart, you can see clearly when the two are in line with each other. Then slide your hands back along the shaft without turning the club, and your hands will automatically be in the right position.

Two key ingredients in any grip are that it should feel comfortable and that it should give you the best control of the club. The hands should be as close together as possible, with the left thumb not visible, almost as if your hands had been glued together to form one hand.

No matter what grip you use, it is also important that the "Vs," formed between the thumbs and the base of the forefingers, are lined up one on top of the other. Only if these "Vs" are in proper alignment will you be able to square the clubface at the moment of impact.

It is essential that you not grip the club too tightly. If you do try to throttle it, two things are likely to occur on your backswing: (1) Your left arm will bend badly, and (2) you won't be able to cock your wrists. The pressure you use in gripping the club should be the same as it would be if you were holding a bird, just tightly enough to keep its wings against its body.

Stance. The most important single element in a good stance is that you should feel comfortable and relaxed when you are addressing the ball, not straining and tense. To achieve this relaxation, you must be standing the proper distance from the ball, neither crowding it, nor reaching for it. Feet should be about shoulder-width apart, but this may vary with the height of the person.

Most people stand too far away from the ball. There is a way to stop yourself from doing this. Because a person will swing more naturally when there is no ball to focus on, take a practice swing just hard enough to make a mark on the ground. Reach down and put a tee behind your left foot. Tee up a ball where you made the mark and address it with your left heel up against the tee. You should now be about the right distance away.

If you want to check whether you're the right distance away from the ball, let the clubhead fall to the ground between your legs. That point on the shaft where the grip starts should be lying somewhere near your left heel.

Your knees should be relaxed with the weight on the balls of the feet, like any athlete about to move into action. A good stance should give you both balance and direction.

To make sure you aim the ball correctly, it might help to approach it from the rear, not from the side, looking from it to the target on a straight line. Once you have taken your stance, you can easily determine whether you're lining up properly by laying a club on the ground next to your toes. Is the end of the club pointing directly at the target? Remember, it doesn't matter how far you hit the ball, if you're aiming in the wrong direction. "Long and wrong" is the name for it.

Swing. The first important thing to remember when starting the backswing is to take the clubhead back straight. One way to do this is the "railroad-track" approach, in which you imagine that you are standing on one track and bringing the clubhead back along the other track and as close to it as possible. You can also place two clubs parallel on the ground and bring the clubhead back between them, making sure in the course of your swing that your clubhead does not cross either club at an angle.

The second vital ingredient in a good golf swing is making a proper shoulder turn. The most common fault in the average swing is trying to hit the ball solely with the hands and arms. But power is generated by the coiling action of a shoulder turn.

As you are addressing the ball, think of the point of each shoulder and the two hands gripped together as being three points that form a triangle. When you start your backswing, the whole triangle should move, not just the hands and arms. For when the hands and arms begin to take control of the club, the body stops turning.

Arnold Palmer has said that the first 12 inches of the backswing are the most important part of your entire swing. That's probably because it is in that first foot that you have to: (1) bring the clubhead back straight, (2) keep it low to the ground without picking it up, (3) establish the whole tempo of your swing, and (4) start turning your shoulders as the clubhead starts back.

To get the feel of a good shoulder turn, put a club behind your back and hold it there by the crooks of your elbows. Make a backswing and hold it at the top. The end of the club should be pointing down at the ball, with the left knee bent toward the right knee. There has to be a slight pause at the top of your swing because you are changing directions.

If you find that your weight is still back on your right foot when you finish the swing—"fire and fall back!"—try gripping the club as you would a baseball bat and hit an imaginary baseball. Now gradually lower the arc of your

111

swing until the clubhead is close to the ground. Keep your head still and swing a golf club the same way.

To make sure you are transferring weight properly, look down over your right shoulder when you complete your follow-through. You should be able to see the back of your right shoe, and your right knee should be touching your left knee.

Try to get the overall feeling that you're swinging *through* the ball, not directing the clubhead *at* it.

Over the next few weeks, I tried to give Harvey some additional pointers out on the course on how to save strokes. He would still regress to his old form now and then, but those moments became fewer and fewer. He was gaining confidence, and he learned something new every time.

One day, on the fourth hole, Harvey was in the right rough, about 180 yards from the green with an acceptable lie. I thought his choice of a 5-wood was a sensible one. But he hit only the top of the ball, and it rolled about 20 yards, still in the rough.

"I really have trouble with that shot," he complained. "I never seem to get all of the ball."

"That's because you're not getting down to it," I told him. "I realize that I told you it was important to sweep the clubhead back low to the ground."

He nodded. "That's what I tried to do."

"Well, this is one instance where you might make an exception to that advice. Since the most important thing is getting down to the ball and hitting it flush, one way to do that is to pick up the clubhead quickly when you swing. If you do that, chances are you'll come down the same way and get down to the ball. It may cut your distance a bit, but you'll get the ball up into the air."

He tried to hit his next shot that way and exaggerated

a bit. Still, the ball popped up in the air and went about 145 yards, just short of the green.

"Keep practicing that shot from the rough," I told him. "You'll soon get the feel of how fast to pick up the clubhead."

Later that day, on the fifteenth hole, Harvey had a 25-foot putt. Although he stroked the ball well, he still left it about 7 feet short of the pin.

"Damn," he said. "I thought I hit that hard enough."

"You were going against the grain."

"I was? How can you tell?"

"Harvey, on this particular course, the grain on every green runs toward the Taconic Parkway. Whatever green you are on, try and locate the parkway, and you'll know whether you're putting with or against the green."

"Is that true on every course?"

"Not always. But if you're not sure on a particular green which way the grain runs, sweep the blade of your putter lightly across the green. If the clubhead moves smoothly with no pull, you're probably going with the grain. But if you feel some slight opposition, like you're rubbing your hand against the stubble of a beard, then you're probably going against, or across, the grain."

On another day, Harvey had hit two good shots on the fourth hole. Then he stubbed his chip shot. I threw another ball down and told him to hit a practice shot.

"You missed that last one because your weight was on your right and you jabbed at it. This time keep your weight toward the left and your hands slightly ahead of the club. Hit the ball without bending your left hand."

He aimed and hit the ball 2½ feet from the pin. But he missed the putt when he pushed it to the right.

"Try it again." I put a tee in the green about an inch and a half behind his putter. "Take the blade back straight and knock the ball in the hole without touching the tee."

This forced him to take a very short backswing and make a good follow-through. The ball went in the center of the cup.

On the eighth hole, Harvey had an uphill lie for his 6-iron shot to the green. He hit it well, but it hooked way to the left.

"Gawd!" he said in awe. "I never thought I would see the day when old Harvey would *hook* the ball."

"You had an uphill lie," I reminded him. "There's a tendency for everyone to hook from that kind of lie. You were smart enough to choke up on the club, but you didn't play for the hook and aim to the right. On the other hand, when you have a downhill lie, you have to bend your knees more, to get down to the ball, and aim to the left because there's a tendency to fade the ball."

On another day, just after we started the second nine, Harvey began to hit all his short irons to the left. His swing looked all right, and I didn't think he was pulling the ball. It had to be the way he was lining up.

"Harvey, I think you're aiming to the left with those shots," I said. "Try doing this. After you look the shot over, plant your right foot first, check it to make sure it's at right angles to the target, then bring your left foot up into position."

He tried it this way a few times, and his aim definitely improved.

And always I kept hammering into his mind those bits of knowledge that he had to learn to be conscious of all the time:

• When you're in a trap, think of hitting a small pie with a marshmallow on top of it—and follow through, follow through.

• Don't squeeze the club. You're holding a bird.

• What's your hurry? Remember, golf is a game of seconds, with long walks in between. Make those seconds count.

• Take the clubhead straight back, not to the inside.

• When you're putting, keep your head absolutely still.

• Distance is far less important than direction, so you don't have to swing hard.

• When in doubt as to which club to use, take the longer one.

• Every time you forget to think about how and where you are going to hit a shot, it's going to cost you strokes.

• Don't lunge at the ball. Pretend you're swinging a rock at the end of a string.

• Are you reaching for the ball, or are you standing comfortably?

• Don't hit "bad-risk" shots. Ask yourself what you will gain by "going for it."

• When you're in a fairway trap, pull out an iron. It's much easier to hit than a wood.

• Don't forget to take the wind into account. It can change a "pussycat" hole into a saber-toothed tiger.

• Pay no attention to what the other guy is hitting. Use the club that's right for you.

• Remember, the most common fault of high-handicap golfers is trying to hit the ball using only their hands and arms. To play good golf, you *have* to make a shoulder turn.

At one point we were asked to play through a slow foursome. I was pleased to see that Harvey took his time, lining up the shot carefully, concentrating on what he was doing, and swinging easily. The ball sailed down the middle of the fairway about 210 yards out, and there were murmurs of approval from the watching foursome. Harvey winked at me as we left the tee.

And promptly topped his 4-iron about 60 yards. "What the hell did I do wrong then?" he snarled.

"You lifted up, and one of the reasons you looked up

115

was that you hadn't prepared yourself mentally for the shot. You were still back gloating on the tee."

"What do you mean 'prepared myself mentally'?"

"All right, tell me this. Without looking, is there a trap on the right or the left of the green?"

He thought for a moment. "On the left."

"Is it a small or a big trap?"

"Ah . . . small."

"Is there any water near the green?"

"Water? I don't think so."

"Does the green slope in any direction?"

He squinted in concentration. "I don't know," he said finally.

"You can look now. If you had really prepared yourself for that shot, you would have formed a mental image of what is up ahead: A large green, sloping from back to front, with a huge, yawning trap in *front* of it, and a small brook about twenty yards behind it. But because you didn't know what was up there, you couldn't resist looking quickly to see where your ball ended up. There's an old saying, Harvey, that when you look up too soon to see what happened, you're not going to like the results."

On another occasion, we were playing the thirteenth hole. It's the hardest hole on the back nine, a 432-yard par-four. Harvey had hit a tremendous drive, about 235 yards to the right side of the fairway. He pulled out a 3-iron and swung as hard as he could, grunting with the effort. The huge divot went almost as far as the ball.

"Harvey, that's a three-iron you're holding, not a cannon. How far do you think you can hit it?"

"After that terrific drive, I wanted to get home in two, Goddamn it!" he said angrily.

"But this is a par-five for you, remember?"

He didn't say anything, just clamped his jaws around

his cigar. When we reached his ball, he still had about 175 yards left.

"Do me a favor, will you, Harvey? Take that same three-iron. Now imagine that you have a six-iron in your hands. You can't possibly reach the green from here with a six-iron, so all you want to do is move the ball closer. Swing just as you would with a six-iron."

He swung easily, going back about as far as he would have to hit an easy 6-iron, and hit the ball cleanly. It landed short of the green and trickled onto the right side of it.

"I barely touched that," he said in amazement.

"And it went a hundred seventy-five yards and onto the green. You get the message, my friend? You don't *have* to hit the ball hard."

"I get it," he said, grinning. "If I can only remember it."

On the seventeenth hole, Harvey's ball ended up in the dirt road on the right. Scowling, he pulled a 5-iron from his bag and started toward the ball.

"Where you are is a free lift, Harvey," I told him. "You can move the ball out on the grass. No penalty."

"I can?" He sounded surprised. "Without any penalty?"

I tapped the scorecard. "It says so right here. Didn't you read the local rules?"

"I guess not."

"You should. They give you a lot of information and some good tips." I then told him how some of the local rules on various courses had helped me, such rules as:

• Drainage ditches—free lift.
• Balls embedded in fairway may be lifted, cleaned, and dropped.
• Yellow stakes at right of fairway are 150 yards from center of green.

117

• If wires crossing fairways are hit, player may replay ball with no penalty.

• Free lift of two club lengths from any man-made installation (poles, utility sheds, pipes, and so forth).

• Solitary large bush on left of fairway is 200 yards from tee.

• Free lift from brook on fifteenth hole *only* on one's drive.

I told Harvey that studying the local rules in advance was basic common sense to help you score.

"Every golf course is different, so knowing the rules for each course can really save you strokes," I told him. "It's just one more way you have to learn to think on the golf course."

Harvey and I played twice a week through the rest of the summer and into the fall. By Labor Day, about half of Harvey's scores were below 90, and by the end of September, three-quarters of them were 89 or under. He reverted occasionally and came in with a horrendous score, but he was still breaking 90 consistently.

One Friday afternoon late in September, Harvey had come in with his best score so far, an 84. Over a beer in the nineteenth hole, I said to him, "I think you're ready for Pinehurst Number Two."

He looked dubious. "I've done some reading, Frank. That's one helluva tough golf course."

"It is. It's considered one of the ten most challenging courses in the world. And if you can break ninety there, you can break it *anywhere*."

"But can I?" There was doubt in his voice, but his eyes were aglow. I knew then that he damn well wanted to try.

"The World Open is on this weekend, and it's played on Number Two Course. You can get some idea of the layout of the course by watching it on TV. I'll make reservations for the four-day package from October 13 through 16, if that's OK with you."

"Sounds great."

"Remember, we're going down there for one reason only: To have you break ninety. Nothing else matters, the food, the entertainment, the scenery. Only the conquest of that golf course. We have to plan for it just as we would for a battle."

"Assault on Number Two," he said, chuckling.

"Exactly. I've taken you as far as I can. Now it's up to you, Harvey."

"Thanks a lot, pal." He gave me a sardonic look. "You know, I feel just like a guy who's been given a million dollars and told he has to spend it all in three days."

"How's that?"

He sighed. "I don't know where to start."

10

Assault on Number Two

*Golf is a game the aim of which is to hit a small ball
into an even smaller hole with weapons singularly
ill-designed for the purpose.*

—Sir Winston Churchill

We started on the plane going down. I had been at the
Pinehurst Hotel and Country Club a number of times and
had brought back scorecards for each of the five courses there.
Since we were going to concentrate exclusively on Number
Two, I gave Harvey the scorecard for that course.

"I've crossed out the indicated yardages from the championship tees because we won't be using them," I told him.
"It's mainly the pros and those competing in the North-
South Amateur who play from the back tees. The vast majority of people play Number Two from the middle tees, and
so will we. Believe me, that's going to be enough of a chal-
lenge. There's no need to make your task impossible."

After studying the scorecard, Harvey said in a surprised voice, "Only six thousand six hundred and eighteen yards? That's not very long."

"No, it's not very long, although it stretches to well over seven thousand yards when you play it from the back tees."

"Yet even from the middle tees you say it's that hard?"

"Harvey, you are going to be surprised when you actually see the course. For one thing, it is not the kind of course, from tee to green, that will overwhelm you like, say, the Monster at Concord, or Firestone, both of which are just plain long. Nor is the course as dramatic as Pebble Beach, or as beautifully groomed as the Augusta National. Pinehurst Number Two is basically a seaside course moved inland. The average person is used to lush green fairways and rough and relatively flat greens. Pinehurst Two looks almost scrubby by comparison. The fairways are watered sparingly, the rough never. The tough wire grass in the rough is not even fertilized. It's just there. In the woods beyond the rough, there is sandy soil covered by pine needles. The pros can come off that kind of surface without much trouble, but it gives amateurs fits. Let's face it, if you stray off the fairway on that course, you're going to pay through the nose for it."

"And that's what makes it so difficult?"

I smiled. "Harvey, I haven't even mentioned the real menace on Number Two Course."

"What's that?"

"The greens. Once you reach the greens, or the area around them, your problems really begin."

"Oh, come on, Frank," Harvey protested. "I've putted on tricky greens before."

"You have never even *seen* greens contoured like these, let alone putted on them. You have to realize that when Donald Ross designed and built the Number Two Course

121

PINEHURST
NUMBER 2

To present competitors with a variety of challenges to test every type of shot which a golfer of championship ability should be qualified to play. This was the dictum renowned Scottish golf course architect Donald J. Ross kept in mind when creating what he called "...the fairest test of championship golf that I have ever designed." The result is Pinehurst Number Two, long recognized as one of the top ten golf courses in the country.

Hole	Back (Rating–73.0)	Middle (Rating–71.0)	Men's Par	Handicap			+/–			Women's (Rating–74.0)	Women's Par	Handicap
10	596	565	5	2						452	5	2
11	434	385	4	8						352	4	10
12	423	405	4	10						344	4	12
13	378	356	4	14						314	4	14
14	444	417	4	4						392	5	6
15	206	183	3	16						154	3	16
16	504	466	5	12						407	5	4
17	187	165	3	18						142	3	18
18	433	388	4	8						350	4	8
In	3605	3330	36							2907	37	
Tot	7051	6618	72							5850	74	
Net Score												

Hole	Back (Rating–73.0)	Middle (Rating–71.0)	Men's Par	Handicap			+/–			Women's (Rating–74.0)	Women's Par	Handicap
1	414	383	4	11						356	4	9
2	454	432	4	3						391	4	7
3	345	331	4	13						299	4	13
4	532	500	5	5						439	5	3
5	438	431	4	1						402	5	1
6	216	206	3	15						186	3	15
7	398	385	4	9						319	4	11
8	487	464	5	7						428	5	5
9	162	156	3	17						123	3	17
Out	3446	3288	36							2943	37	

Date_____Scorer_____Attest_____

over fifty years ago, there was no sophisticated equipment or machinery available. Using only a horse, a cart, a shovel, and a rake, Donald Ross built it all by hand. Every contour of every green was handmade, and every green has four-way drainage. It can rain all night long, and the next morning you won't even get your feet wet on the greens. Today, with all our equipment and knowledge, we have a hell of a time providing four-way drainage. Ross did it all by hand. And, mainly because he was a Scotsman himself, Pinehurst Number Two comes as close to matching golf courses in Scotland as any course in this country."

"OK. I'm impressed," Harvey said, grinning. "I'll take the guided tour. When does the bus leave?"

"Never mind. You'll find out what I mean when you start counting your strokes around the green area."

"Is it really that tricky?"

"It is, believe me. Because it's not only the difficulty you have reading and putting on the greens, it's getting to the damn things in the first place. Mounds or swales or traps are in front of most of them, and almost every one falls away at the edges. Sam Snead puts this course at the top of his list of U.S. courses, because, as he says, 'You won't see any pitch-and-putt scramblers winning there. You've got to hit every shot on old Number Two.' "

"What are you trying to do—brainwash me?"

"No, just warning you not to underestimate the course when you first see it. It looks almost easy. But you're going to have to concentrate as hard as you can on your short game. Chipping to those greens can be a nightmare."

"Why?"

"Because it's so devilishly hard to read the contours. On most other courses you can get away with a bad chip shot. But on Number Two, if you mishit a chip, your ball will probably roll right off the green. On no other course that I've played—and I've played hundreds—is 'touch' around the green so important."

"Is it Bermuda or Bent grass?"

"You get a break there. About three years ago, they changed from Bermuda to Bent, which should help you some. Bent grass holds shots a little better and will usually putt a little truer."

"Thank the Lord for small favors."

That evening, after a late dinner at the Pinehurst Hotel, I picked up the special red phone in the lobby which is connected to the starting-time office. A few days earlier, I had spoken to Bill Dowling, Diamondhead Corporation's Director of Marketing, explaining the purpose of our visit, and he had promised to arrange starting times for us on Number Two Course for all four days of our stay. There are five courses at Pinehurst, and all of them require starting tee-off times for every player. So, each night, the phone is continually ringing in the starting-time office as the guests call in to express their course preference for the next day and are given starting times on that course.

Our tee-off time was confirmed and I said to Harvey, "We go off at nine fifteen. Twosomes are usually paired with other twosomes, but under the circumstances we can go off by ourselves."

"Special compensation?" Harvey grinned. "There aren't going to be any distractions, huh?"

"That's right. The next two days have to be a crash course on the mysteries of Number Two."

"To get me ready for the final assault?"

"Exactly. Thursday and Friday you'll go for score, the magic number. Did you get a little notebook?"

"I got it, but what exactly goes into it?"

"You put in it every scrap of information you can gather about each hole: Yardages to the green from a certain rock

125

or tree; placement of traps; whether to be right or left on a hole; the smart way to play each hole; and, above all, how to cope with the greens."

"Just like the pros."

"Just like the pros. Now let's get some sleep, Nicklaus."

I had left a wake-up call for 7 A.M., and by the time we finished breakfast and were driven the few hundred yards to the main clubhouse, it was 8:20. We registered and walked outside. The scene there has to be described.

Imagine, if you will, a mechanized army of ants suddenly turned loose in a new territory, whizzing back and forth along paths, each intent on some vital purpose. I had never in my life seen so many golf carts in motion in one place. There were literally hundreds of them, all filled with eager golfers from all over the United States, frantic to get to the proper tee at their assigned times. The first tees of all five courses were within easy walking (or carting) distance from the clubhouse, and on that cool, clear October morning, it was evident that each and every visitor was determined not to waste a precious minute of this special golfing experience. Pinehurst, North Carolina, was living up to its reputation as one of the golf meccas of the world.

After Harvey and I had obtained a cart for ourselves, we drove up to the enormous practice tee. It was jammed. The usual routine there, we discovered, was to park your golf cart in line in front of the first tee of your preselected course, check in with the starter, and hit some practice balls during the waiting period. We had left ourselves a good half-hour, so I went to check in with the starter on Number Two while Harvey loosened up on the practice tee. Then I joined him there.

As we stood on the first tee of Number Two Course, I turned to Harvey. "We won't even keep score today. Concentrate on familiarizing yourself with each hole and filling up your notebook with useful information and reminders, anything that will help you play every hole as knowledgeably and smartly as you can."

"That's no fun—not keeping score." He sounded like a little boy who had just been refused permission to go to the movies.

"Harvey, do you want to break ninety?"

"Damn right!"

"If you start keeping score, you won't be concentrating one hundred percent on *how* to play each hole. You'll be thinking how many. Do it my way, will you?"

He smiled ruefully. "OK, teach. I'll be a good boy."

During the next two days, Harvey really came to grips with the course. We played Number Two twice each day, morning and afternoon. Harvey learned the smart way to play each hole and the things in particular to watch out for. His notebook began to fill up with distances to the green from various spots in the fairway and rough, which traps to avoid at all costs, and the lay of the land around each green.

About the first hole, a 383-yard par-four, he had written: "383 yards. Fairway bunker out 225 yards on left. Hit driver, aiming at bunker and let ball drift right to fairway. Bunker 160 yards from green. There is bunker to left of green and one 30 yards short and to the right. Better to be over right-hand trap and short of green than over. If over, difficult chip to table top where ball will roll to front of green or off it. *Important:* Stay away from deep, left-hand trap."

Harvey also found out soon enough about the contours of the greens. After three-putting his third green, he shook his head in exasperation. "That ball broke about six inches, and I didn't even *see* a break at all. These greens are impossible to read."

"It broke right near the cup, and you didn't look at the run of the grain around the cup," I told him.

127

First Hole. *Not too difficult an opening hole. The toughest pin placement is on the left side of the green. Mounds on the right of the green present some delicate chipping. In the 1975 World Open, Jack Nicklaus defeated Billy Casper in a sudden-death play-off on this hole.*

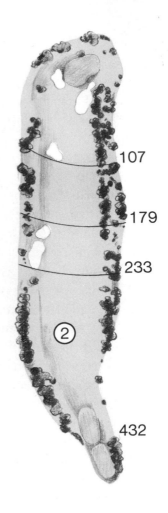

107

179

233

②

432

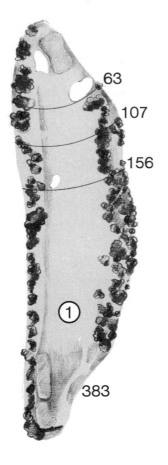

63

107

156

①

383

Second Hole. *A tough par-four, with bunkers on the left in the driving area. In the final round of the 1971 Club Professional Championship, Sam Snead hit a 2-iron 8 inches from the cup for a birdie— and an eventual win.*

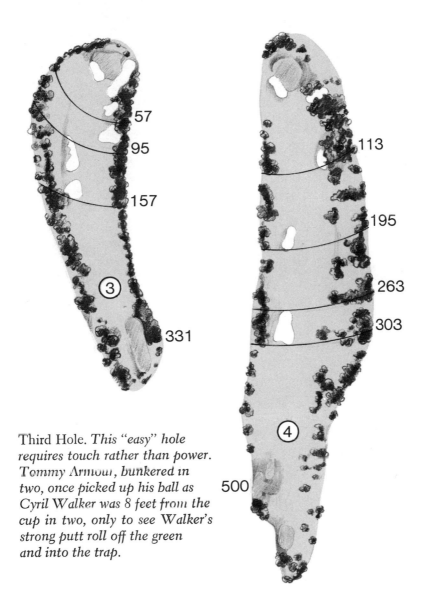

57

95

157

③

331

195

113

263

303

④

500

Third Hole. *This "easy" hole requires touch rather than power. Tommy Armour, bunkered in two, once picked up his ball as Cyril Walker was 8 feet from the cup in two, only to see Walker's strong putt roll off the green and into the trap.*

Fourth Hole. *On this hole, Billy Joe Patton drove deep in the woods, but sliced it back onto the fairway and made a "birdie when I was really dead" for a victory in the 1962 North-South Amateur. The World Golf Hall of Fame stands behind the fourth green.*

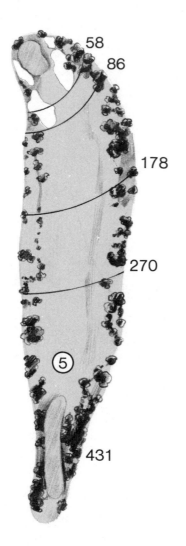

58
86
178
270
⑤
431

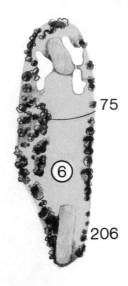

75
⑥
206

Sixth Hole. *Swales in front of the green require full carry to it. In the 1973 World Open, Tom Watson hit his drive out of bounds here—the day after he had shot a record-equaling 62.*

Fifth Hole. *This is the toughest hole on the course, and a birdie here will be well earned. Jack Nicklaus has bogeyed and double-bogeyed this hole more than any other on the Number Two Course.*

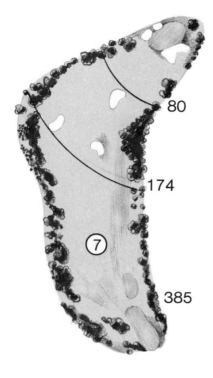

80

174

⑦

385

Seventh Hole. *This deceptively
difficult par-four is the only
hole Gibby Gilbert bogeyed
in his course-record-setting
round of 62 in the 1973 World
Open.*

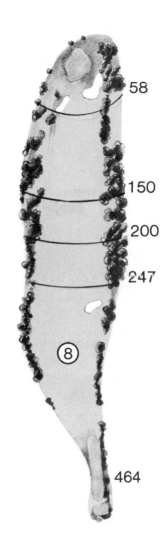

58

150

200

247

⑧

464

Eighth Hole. *Arnold Palmer
played this hole only once
in his scheduled two-round
North-South Amateur semi-
final in 1949, as Frank
Stranahan closed him out 12
and 11.*

156

Ninth Hole. *At the 1950 North and South Open, this hole became a partner in the notorious Hole-in-One Orgy, as it yielded two aces within an hour while the fifteenth hole was giving up two more.*

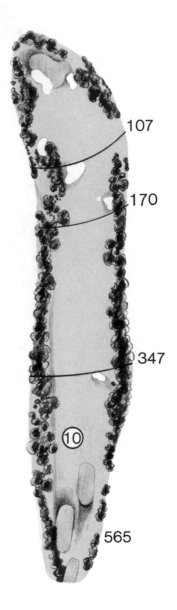

107

170

347

565

Tenth Hole. *The longest hole on the course, with a narrow opening through the swales. Miller Barber's birdie here helped him win the 1973 World Open—and claim golf's richest prize ever, $100,000.*

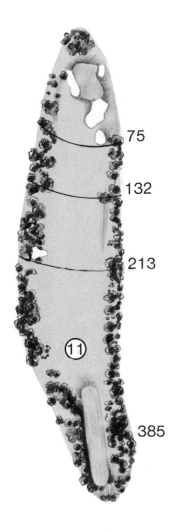

75

132

213

⑪

385

Twelfth Hole. *George Burns, defending his 1974 North-South Amateur Champion-ship, birdied this hole in both his morning and afternoon rounds, after hitting into the same fairway bunker each time.*

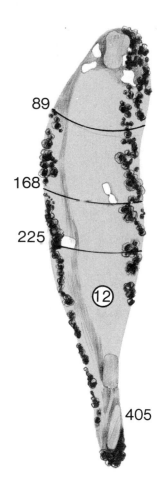

89

168

225

⑫

405

Eleventh Hole. *In 1940, Ben Hogan struck what has been termed "the most significant shot ever hit at Pinehurst" when he exploded from a bunker for a birdie—and launched the Age of Hogan.*

Thirteenth Hole. *Greenside bunkers make certain pin placements here very testing. Billy Casper's birdie on this hole in the 1975 World Open shot him into strong contention.*

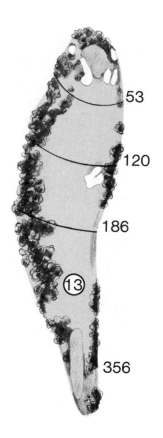

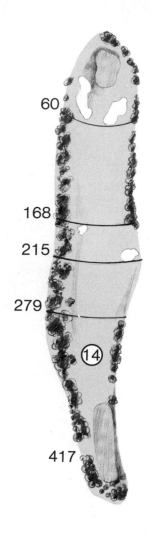

Fourteenth Hole. *In the 1973 World Open, Tom Watson hit an 8-iron here for an eagle. He followed that with four straight birdies—and still lost to Miller Barber.*

183

Fifteenth Hole. *It's all carry here with a hollow in front of the green. In 1974, Curtis Strange hit 3-irons for birdies in both his morning and afternoon rounds to win the North-South Amateur— by two.*

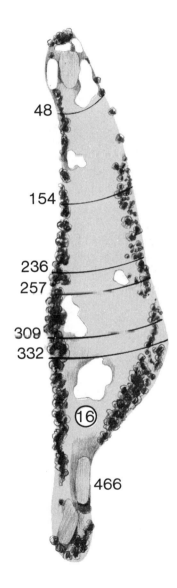

48

154

236
257

309
332

466

Sixteenth Hole. *On this, the only water hole on the course, Johnny Miller hit a 3-wood 10 feet from the pin and two-putted to defeat Frank Beard and Nicklaus in a play-off in the 1974 World Open.*

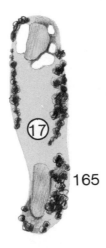

165

Seventeenth Hole. *On this well-bunkered par-three, Dutch Harrison was one member of a threesome that scored a total of five strokes—a hole-in-one and two birdies.*

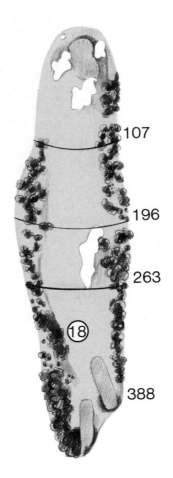

107

196

263

388

Eighteenth Hole. *In 1959, a chubby nineteen-year-old sank a 6-foot putt on this tough finishing hole to win the North-South Amateur title. His name? Jack Nicklaus.*

"Look at the what?"

"You've watched a lot of golf tournaments on television, Harvey. Have you ever seen the pros walk over to the cup and look down into it?"

"Yes. Plenty of times."

"What do you think they're looking for?"

He thought for a moment. "The condition of the cup? Whether it's tilted or damaged?"

"That's only about ten percent of it. What they are most concerned about is the way the grain of the grass runs around the cup area. The cup is fresh cut vertically every day. If you look closely at it, you can see where the grass runners are loose because their growth has been interrupted. That will tell you the direction of the grain in the pin area and which way the ball will break at that point. And that's where it matters. When you hit a thirty-foot putt, you're not worried about what the grain will do to the ball for the first twenty-five or twenty-six feet. It's in the last four feet, when the ball begins to die near the cup, that the grain will begin to affect it. And on Number Two Course, the breaks on the green are so subtle and the pin placements so diabolically chosen that you need all the help you can get."

I was able to counsel Harvey in a few other areas as well, such as helping him gauge distances for entry into his notebook and making him aware of the danger of going for the pin on certain holes. But mainly it was a matter of reminding him of things I had mentioned earlier.

For example, on the par-five, 500-yard fourth hole, Harvey had a 7-iron left to the green for his third shot—and promptly pushed it way to the right.

I said, "Remember what happens when you have a shot in which the ball is lower than your feet?"

He nodded in sudden understanding. "The tendency is to push it—and on that shot the ball *was* lower than my feet."

"Right on. Better mark it down in your book to remind yourself."

During the morning round on the second day, I made some special notes of my own, and at lunch I trotted them out.

"I still don't think you fully understand that you are going to have to solve those greens if you're going to score well. I kept track of the number of shots it took you to get down when you were within thirty yards of the hole," I told him. "What do you think the total was?"

"I don't know," he admitted, "but I wasn't chipping and putting that badly."

"Not badly, but not good enough either, Harvey. An acceptable number of strokes from that distance or shorter would be about two and a half shots per hole, or a total of forty-five. You took a fat fifty-five, and that many will keep you above ninety every time."

So, after lunch, we had a pitch-and-chip session—for well over an hour. The afternoon round showed a marked improvement in his short game. He was concentrating more now and hitting the ball firmly and smoothly.

But Thursday morning, when we stood on the first tee, ready to go for the magic number, Harvey was visibly nervous.

"Relax, Harvey," I told him. "After two full days on old Number Two, you know the course pretty well."

"I wonder," he shook his head. "Those damn greens."

"Look at it this way," I said, trying to reassure him. "When you first came here, Number Two Course was an enemy alien. Now it's more like an old friend. Don't try to subdue it. It's a friend. Go along with it. Humor it. Adapt yourself to all of its quirks. You know it well enough by now to do that."

His first drive restored his confidence, with the ball ending up in the middle of the fairway about 220 yards out. He hit his 5-iron a little heavy and was short of the green. His chip was firm, a little too firm, but he got down in two. Not a bad start.

Harvey played the 432-yard, par-four second hole just right—for him. That is, he played it as a par-five, which it was —for him. He hit an easy 3-wood off the tee, aiming left, and the ball faded into the right center of the fairway. His 5-iron second shot landed just short of the trap in front of the green. Remembering not to aim for the pin, which was sitting on top of a mound and would have taken his ball way over, he hit a soft wedge to the left center of the green. Two putts for "his" par.

"Nice work, Harvey," I told him. "You played that perfectly. Keep it up."

He did—and he didn't. The short par-four third hole has been described as a hole that "lulls you to sleep." It seems so damn easy, only 331 yards. Maybe Harvey felt the same way. Whatever the reason, he eased up, or lost concentration, or whatever, and took a seven on the hole. The rest of the nine, he hit some good shots, but a few too many poor ones, and ended up with a 46.

As we were having a snack at the Halfway House, he asked, "What did I get on the front nine?"

I looked at him steadily. "I don't think it's a good idea to tell you. It won't help and it could hurt. Just play the back nine as well as you can."

Which was pretty good indeed—six, five, five, four, five, four, five for the first seven holes. When he stepped up to the seventeenth tee, he took a deep breath and asked, ever so casually, "What do I need on these last two holes to break ninety, Frank?"

I hesitated and he turned to me. "I just gotta know."

"I still don't think it's a good idea for you to know, Harvey."

139

His jaw set. "I wanna know. Tell me. What do I need?"

I sighed. It was his game and his score. "A bogey on each hole will do it."

"Two bogeys," he said happily. "That's duck soup."

Duck soup indeed! On the 165-yard, par-three seventeenth hole, Harvey hit his 5-iron off the toes—smack into the trap short of the green. Out of the trap and over the green. Chip back on. Two putts. A double bogey.

As he stood on the eighteenth tee, realizing that he now had to get a par here, I could see him tensing. The eighteenth is a tough finishing hole. It was going to be a disaster, I thought.

And it was—a complete disaster. From tee to trap to rough to woods to trap—plus three putts. He took a nine and he was crushed. Ninety-four blows!

"It was partly my fault, Harvey," I tried to console him. "Even when you asked, I shouldn't have told you what you had to get. It put unnecessary pressure on you. The last two holes are hard enough by themselves. They deserve all your attention."

"I played damn good until I blew it," he said angrily.

"Tomorrow," I said. "Tomorrow you're going to play each hole one by one and let me worry about the total. Deal?"

"Deal," he said grimly. "It's my last chance."

The next morning the grimness was gone. He was relaxed and philosophical as we approached the first tee. He had practiced a full hour.

"You know, I'm not going to worry about it," he said, smiling. "If I break ninety, fine. If not, well, I gave it the old college try."

With that attitude, I thought, he just might have a chance.

Harvey's relaxed frame of mind paid off, and he started

the front nine beautifully—bogey, bogey, par, par. It was on the fifth hole, the number-one handicap hole on the course, that he got into trouble. A 431-yard, par-four, the fifth hole had the only blind tee shot on the course.

Harvey's woes occurred mainly because of a simple omission in his notes. He hit a 3-wood off the tee, wisely intending to play the hole as a par-five, and groaned as his ball disappeared in the right-hand woods.

He looked at me, his eyebrows raised. "I hit that pretty good," he said, puzzled. "It had a little fade, but not enough to carry it into the woods. I can't understand it."

"I can. Your navigation was faulty in one crucial respect."

"What's that?"

"Harvey, the tee itself *aims* to the right."

He studied it. "By God, it does. But I lined up with the markers."

"Never believe markers, my friend. Somebody mows the tee and maybe replaces the markers off the line. You come along and believe that they're accurate, and you're automatically in trouble. In pro tournaments, they paint the proper marker placement so that kind of thing can't happen. But this is not a tournament, so you have to make sure you're lined up correctly. You weren't."

Harvey elected to try a shot out of the woods—and hit a tree. It was a bad-risk shot. Although he managed to get out on the next attempt, he was still 220 yards from the green, and he was lying three.

Despite his predicament, Harvey kept his cool. The green on this hole was guarded by two bunkers in front on each side. A well-hit wood could easily have carried him into one of them—and more trouble. But Harvey hit a good 6-iron, then an easy 9-iron to the green. His 25-foot putt stopped 2 inches from the hole. A seven. But it could have been worse.

141

His 3-wood on the 206-yard par-three sixth hole left him short of the green. His chip was too firm for a green that falls away to the rear, and he went over. He stabbed at the next shot, and the ball went 6 inches. Onto the green tentatively, two putts—and another triple bogey.

He was beginning to sweat now, knowing he could not have many more such holes. Rattled, he mishit his drive, and the ball skittered out to the left about 120 yards into the rough. When he reached the ball, he took several deep breaths, trying to regain his composure. His notes told him that the fairway narrowed sharply near the green on this par-four, 385-yard hole, and I was very relieved when he did not pull out a wood. Instead, he hit a good 5-iron out of the rough, then a perfect 8-iron to the green. He gave a yell when his 10-foot putt rolled to the edge of the cup, lingered fractionally, then dropped.

It was the turning point, I think, the moment of truth. After two triple bogeys and a very bad drive, and faced with the strong possibility of still another bad hole, to *still* manage to salvage a par was a marvelous morale booster for him. From that moment on he played with more ease and self-assurance. Oh, he missed some shots and didn't always use his head, but the important thing was that he didn't let those mistakes unnerve him.

On the fifteenth, a 183-yard, par-three hole, he simply made the wrong club selection, even though his notes specifically advised him to "take one more club than you think you need—and stay left." Instead of choosing a 4- or 5-wood, he hit a 4-iron, and the ball bounced right in front of the green and into the huge trap there. He didn't follow through on his trap shot, and the ball stayed in the bunker. He got out on the next shot, but lay 35 feet from the pin. He putted boldly and got down in two. It was an important stroke to save. If he had three-putted, it would have meant a triple bogey and would possibly have eroded his confidence just when he needed it most—on the pressure-filled finishing three holes.

He played the relatively easy par-five sixteenth hole very carefully and safely, and made par by dropping a 5-foot putt. When once again he stood on the fateful seventeenth tee, all he needed was a total of ten strokes on the last two holes to break 90—a bogey and a double bogey.

"I'm not going to ask you what I have to get on these last two holes," he said. "Just tell me if it's possible."

"Yes. It's possible. Just play them one by one, Harvey."

On the par-three, 165-yard seventeenth, Harvey's notes read: "Trouble in front. Get it *on* the green. You can't play this one cute. Better long than short."

Normally, he would have selected a 5- or 6-iron. But after studying his notes and testing the wind (very slightly crosswind), he hit a very easy 4-iron to the back edge of the green, some 40 feet from the pin. But this time he did three-putt for a bogey, and his expression was sober as he strode to the eighteenth tee.

About the eighteenth, a 388-yard, par-four hole, Harvey had noted: "Stay left off tee. Yawning trap on right. On second shot, either go for green, or play left and short."

Swinging easily, he hit a driver fairly well to the left, and it slid onto the fairway about 200 yards out. That left him some 185 yards to the green, and it was all carry. Harvey decided to play it safe all the way. He hit a good 6-iron short and to the left, but his pitch shot carried his ball to the upper level of the green and left him with a tricky downhill 45-foot putt.

Trying to baby it, he left it 4 feet short. He studied the putt closely and stood over the ball. I could see his hands trembling slightly. Then he stepped away from the ball and turned to me.

143

"I've got a hunch that I need this putt to break ninety."
He stared at me, waiting for an answer.

"Knock it in, Harvey," I said softly.

He played for about an inch break, hit it firmly, and the ball rammed right into the back of the cup. He started to shout, then looked up quickly. "Well? I didn't blow it again, did I?"

"You didn't even need to make that putt, Harvey," I said, grinning at him. "You got yourself an eighty-eight. Congratulations!"

His own grin was huge. "Son of a gun! How 'bout that? I broke ninety on Pinehurst Number Two."

"You and Johnny Miller."

"How about playing it again? Maybe a little side bet?"

I shook my head. "Harvey, I think you better quit Number Two while you're ahead. We'll try one of the other courses this afternoon."

That evening we celebrated. Harvey had surprised himself and me by shooting an 85 on the Number Three Course. At one point during the evening, he looked me straight in the eye and said, "Frank, I've got this game licked."

I didn't say a word. I didn't have to. Harvey would soon find out what we all have—that *nobody* has this game of golf licked.

Even now, chances are that Jack Nicklaus, probably the greatest golfer ever to play the game, is still wondering why he duck-hooked his drive into the water on the eighteenth hole in the 1975 Canadian Open—and lost the lead and eventually the tournament.

And we are plain mortals by comparison. Oh, well. Playing the game is all that matters. So, as my Latin teacher used to say, *"Ite e via. Veni subito."*

"Get out of my way! Here I come!"